BASIC SKILLS AND BEYOND

MULTIPLICATION & DIVISION

GRADES 4–5

by Jillayne Prince Wallaker

ACTIVITIES SUPPORT THESE LEARNING OUTCOMES

Number Sense and Operations

- Understand place value, equivalencies, and representations of whole numbers, fractions, and decimals
- Understand the meanings and properties of operations
- Develop strategies for accurate methods of computation and estimation

Algebra

- Express quantities and relationships using letters, symbols, and equations
- Model mathematical situations with graphs, tables, and equations

Measurement

- Understand measurable characteristics (e.g., length, area, volume)
- Develop strategies to determine estimates and exact measurements of objects

Carson-Dellosa Publishing Company, Inc. • Greensboro, North Carolina

Credits

Editor:
Amy Gamble

Layout Design and Art Coordination:
Jon Nawrocik

Inside Illustrations:
Ray Lambert

Cover Design:
Peggy Jackson

ISBN 0-88724-183-2

Table of Contents

Introduction & Extensions

Mastering the related skills, multiplication and division, is a prerequisite to many mathematical concepts which will be built upon in later grades. It is essential for students to understand the concept involved, not just memorize the facts associated with these two functions. For this reason, both multiplication and division are presented in a variety of ways in this book.

The first step to understanding is through concept building using manipulatives to model multiplication and division problems. This book includes pages that assist in bridging from concrete to abstract. The bridges are made by having students picture the problems using sketches and arrays. Although we do not want students to rely on pictures, we do want them to build their understanding of the concrete.

Also included are pages that encourage students to see the relationships between multiplication and division as well as other concepts such as addition, subtraction, counting by multiples, etc. Strategy building such as multiplication boxes, repeated addition, the relationships between ones, tens, and hundreds, etc., are also provided. If a number of strategies for solving a problem are presented, the probability of a child understanding the concept and successfully mastering the process is greatly increased.

The final step is to allow the student to bring her understanding of multiplication and division to other areas of mathematics, such as story problems, geometry, algebra, riddles, etc. Students are also challenged to demonstrate mastery by designing and writing their own problems. The following suggestions are ways to enhance and individualize the activities in this book.

1. Allow students to work with partners and use pictures or manipulatives to work out problems they do not agree on.
2. Make arrays or sketches for students of problems that are incorrect. Visualizing the problem will allow students to understand the problem, become more accurate, and even memorize the fact.
3. Have students write the fact families for the problems presented.
4. Have students talk through with a partner or write their thinking processes for various problems. Often verbalizing assists understanding.
5. Ask students to use a page from the book as a model to write their own problems. Placed on 3 x 5 index cards with the answers on the back, these are great student-made additions to a math center.
6. Explore the idea of odd and even factors and products. How does this relate to dividends, divisors, and quotients? Encourage students to find patterns.
7. Show students examples of real-life arrays, such as food containers, ice cube trays, packing containers, etc.

Name ______________________ Date __________

Problem Search

Basic Facts

Directions: Find and circle the multiplication and division equations in the puzzle. They can be horizontal, vertical, or diagonal. Write the problems and their partners on the lines below. The first one has been done for you.

3	X	3	=	9	27	12	16	49	32	64	2	9
12	2	6	6	36	4	8	7	56	8	70
9	36	54	18	7	4	3	40	7	52	8
32	8	4	2	2	2	8	16	30	12	9
3	7	15	9	27	5	24	6	4	6	62
28	56	5	9	45	10	5	3	48	5	42
21	7	3	81	7	14	7	2	5	7	20
35	72	9	8	5	63	35	25	6	4	22

3 x 3 = 9

9 ÷ 3 = 3

NAME ____________________ DATE __________

ARRAYS OF FACTS

FACT FAMILIES

Directions: Look at each array. Write the two multiplication and two division equations shown by the array.

1. ___ x ___ = ___
   ___ x ___ = ___
   ___ ÷ ___ = ___
   ___ ÷ ___ = ___

2. ___ x ___ = ___
   ___ x ___ = ___
   ___ ÷ ___ = ___
   ___ ÷ ___ = ___

3. ___ x ___ = ___
   ___ x ___ = ___
   ___ ÷ ___ = ___
   ___ ÷ ___ = ___

4. ___ x ___ = ___
   ___ x ___ = ___
   ___ ÷ ___ = ___
   ___ ÷ ___ = ___

5. ___ x ___ = ___
   ___ x ___ = ___
   ___ ÷ ___ = ___
   ___ ÷ ___ = ___

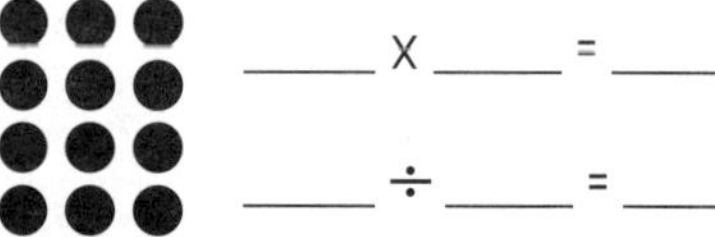

6. ___ x ___ = ___
   ___ x ___ = ___
   ___ ÷ ___ = ___
   ___ ÷ ___ = ___

7. ___ x ___ = ___
   ___ x ___ = ___
   ___ ÷ ___ = ___
   ___ ÷ ___ = ___

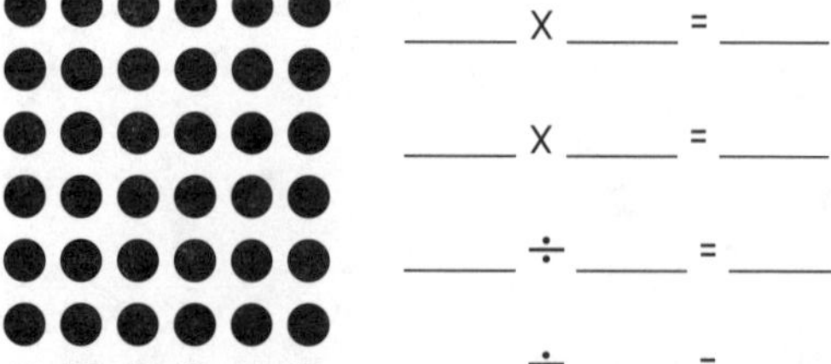

8. ___ x ___ = ___
   ___ x ___ = ___
   ___ ÷ ___ = ___
   ___ ÷ ___ = ___

MIXED PRACTICE

NAME ______________________ DATE __________

TABLE TABULATION

BASIC FACTS

Directions: Complete the multiplication table. Then, use the table to solve the problems below. Circle each answer on the table.

X	0	1	2	3	4	5	6	7	8	9	10
0											
1											
2											
3											
4											
5											
6											
7											
8											
9											
10											

1. 72 = 9 x
2. 30 ÷ 6 =
3. 3 x 6 =
4. ____ = 28 ÷ 4
5. 48 = ____ x 6
6. 24 ÷ 8 =
7. 7 x ____ = 49
8. ____ ÷ 6 = 4
9. 4 x 8 =
10. ____ = 18 ÷ 2
11. 8 ÷ ____ = 8
12. 16 = 4 x
13. 2 x 7 =
14. 3 x ____ = 21
15. 20 = ____ x 5
16. 6 x ____ = 36
17. ____ = 27 ÷ 9
18. 8 x ____ = 40
19. 6 x 7 =
20. 56 = ____ x 7

NAME ____________ DATE ________

RECIPE FOR MATH

MULTIPLICATION

APPLICATION

Directions: Use the recipe to answer the questions. Show your work.

RECIPE

Trail Mix
(serves 2)

Ingredients:

1 individual-sized package of candy-coated chocolate pieces

2 handfuls of peanuts or mixed nuts

3 tablespoons of ring-shaped oat cereal

4 teaspoons of candy corn

5 tablespoons of another cereal of your choice

6 tablespoons of raisins

7 vanilla cookies, broken up

8 bow- or circle-shaped pretzels

9 dried apricots cut into small pieces

Directions:

Place the ingredients in a large bowl. Toss or shake to mix. Store in a sealed container until ready to use.

1. What do you do with this recipe if you need enough for 4 people?

2. If each tablespoon of raisins held 7 raisins, how many raisins would there be in one batch of this trail mix?

3. If each vanilla cookie was broken into 4 pieces, how many pieces of vanilla cookie would be in one batch of trail mix?

4. If each handful of mixed nuts held 9 nuts, how many nuts would be in 2 batches of trail mix?

5. Karen is having 16 friends over. In order to serve Trail Mix to her friends, what does she need to do with this recipe? Write a multiplication problem for each ingredient to show the amounts she needs.

Name ______________________ Date __________

MULTIPLICATION

Find the Winner

Basic Facts

Directions: The first roll is the first factor for each player's five rolls. Each roll is multiplied by the first factor. The five products are added to get a final score.

Game 1: first roll: 

Mikaela's rolls:     

Jeremy's rolls:     

Game 2: first roll: 

Mikaela's rolls:    

Jeremy's rolls:    

Game 3: first roll: 

Mikaela's rolls:     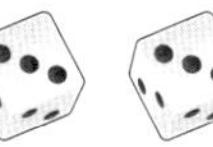

Jeremy's rolls:     

Game 4: first roll: 

Mikaela's rolls:    

Jeremy's rolls:    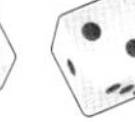

Game 5: first roll: 

Mikaela's rolls:

Jeremy's rolls:     

Game 6: first roll: 

Mikaela's rolls:    

Jeremy's rolls:     

NAME ______________________ DATE __________

MULTIPLICATION

REPEATED ADDITION

CONCEPT DEVELOPMENT

Directions: Show the sets using place value representation. Write the repeated addition sentence and solve. Write the product.

EXAMPLE

Place Value Representation

■ = 1,000 □ = 100

| = 10 • = 1

67
x 2
134

can also be solved using repeated addition:

67 + 67 = 134

||| ⁘ + ||| ⁘

= □ ||| ⁘

1. 86 x 4

2. 74 x 3

3. 93 x 2

4. 51 x 4

5. 35 x 6

6. 22 x 4

7. 47 x 5

8. 382 x 3

9. 269 x 2

10. 144 x 6

11. 428 x 5

12. 547 x 4

NAME ______________________ DATE __________

Tens and Hundreds

MULTIPLICATION

Relationships

Directions: Solve each set of problems. Use your multiplication facts and what you know about place value to help you solve the problems.

1. 5 x 9 =
   5 x 90 =
   5 x 900 =

2. 7 x 3 =
   7 x 30 =
   7 x 300 =

3. 8 x 6 =
   8 x 60 =
   8 x 600 =

4. 9 x 4 =
   9 x 40 =
   9 x 400 =

5. 7 x 7 =
   7 x 70 =
   7 x 700 =

6. 6 x 4 =
   6 x 40 =
   6 x 400 =

7. 4 x 8 =
   4 x 80 =
   4 x 800 =

8. 2 x 3 =
   2 x 30 =
   2 x 300 =

9. 90
   x 8

10. 200
    x 5

11. 40
    x 4

12. 50
    x 9

13. 700
    x 8

14. 30
    x 6

15. 900
    x 2

16. 70
    x 9

Example

4 x 2 =
8

4 x 20 =
80

4 x 200 =
800

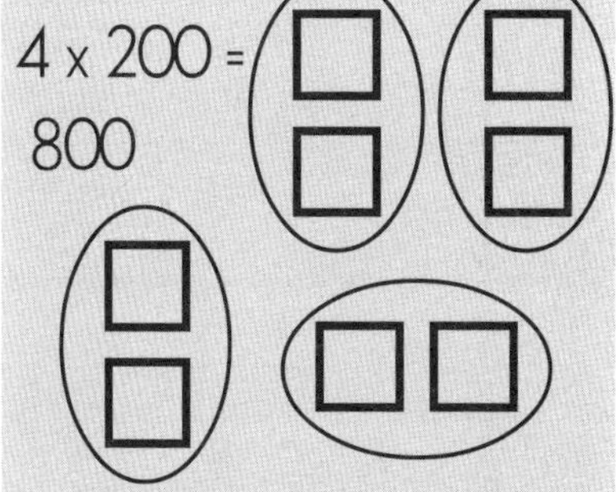

NAME ____________________ DATE __________

MULTIPLICATION

TAKE IT APART

MULTIPLYING 2-DIGIT NUMBERS

Directions: Take each problem apart. Write the two multiplication problems that make up each problem. Solve and add. The final sum is the product.

EXAMPLE

$$\begin{array}{r} 56 \\ \times\ 4 \\ \hline \end{array}$$

is equal to

(4 x 6) + (4 x 50)

4 x 6 = 24

4 x 50 = 200

24 + 200 = 224

so

$$\begin{array}{r} 56 \\ \times\ 4 \\ \hline 224 \end{array}$$

1. 81 x 9
2. 57 x 3
3. 78 x 6
4. 65 x 2
5. 32 x 4
6. 56 x 7
7. 81 x 5
8. 67 x 6
9. 39 x 7
10. 30 x 8
11. 21 x 5
12. 88 x 3
13. 79 x 9
14. 65 x 4
15. 89 x 7

MORE PRACTICE

Explain why you can find the correct product using this strategy.

Name ______________________ Date __________

More Strategy

MULTIPLICATION

Multiplying 2-Digit Numbers

Directions: Take each problem apart. Write the four multiplication problems that make up each problem. The final sum is the product.

Problem	Letter	Problem	Letter
24 x 82	R	51 x 46	I
43 x 47	O	82 x 23	E
65 x 92	C	37 x 56	R
94 x 71	O	68 x 13	U
77 x 26	T	14 x 54	P

Example

27
x 89

is equal to

(9 x 7) + (9 x 20) +
(80 x 7) + (80 x 20)

9 x 7 = 63
9 x 20 = 180
80 + 7 = 560
80 x 20 = 1,600

63 + 180 + 560 +
1,600 = 2,403

so 27
x 89
2,403

More Practice

Arrange the letters according to the corresponding product in order from least to greatest to find out where the world's largest radio telescope is located.

Name ______________________ Date __________

Adjusting the Strategy

Multiplication

Multiplying 2-Digit Numbers

Directions: Take each problem apart. Write the two multiplication problems that make up each problem. Solve and add. The final sum is the product.

1. 71 x 36
2. 58 x 46
3. 42 x 35
4. 19 x 86

Example

65 x 32

is equal to

(2 x 65) + (30 x 65)

2 x 65 = 130

30 x 65 = 1,950

130 + 1,950 = 2,080

so

65 x 32 = 2,080

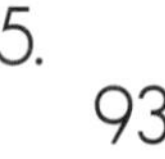

5. 93 x 49
6. 38 x 27
7. 24 x 63
8. 99 x 54

9. 65 x 72
10. 37 x 14
11. 43 x 96
12. 72 x 23

More Practice

Explain why you can find the correct product using this strategy.

NAME ______________________ DATE __________

MULTIPLICATION

SPLITTING BIGGER NUMBERS

MULTIPLYING 3-DIGIT NUMBERS

Directions: Take each problem apart. Write the multiplication problems that make up each problem. Solve and add. The final sum is the product.

1. 606 x 95

2. 350 x 72

3. 490 x 18

4. 861 x 43

5. 907 x 51

6. 831 x 186

7. 347 x 216

8. 257 x 751

9. 946 x 916

10. 895 x 506

EXAMPLES

283 x 43

is equal to

(3 x 283) + (40 x 283)

3 x 283 = 849

40 x 283 = 11,320

849 + 11,320 = 12,169

so 283 x 43 = 12,169

278 x 174

is equal to

(4 x 278) + (70 x 278) + (100 x 278)

NAME ______________________ DATE __________

PLACE VALUE BOXES

MULTIPLICATION

MULTIPLYING 2-DIGIT NUMBERS

Directions: Write the product of the bottom factor and each digit of the top factor in the appropriate place value box. Add along the diagonals to find the final product. Carry to the next box when necessary.

EXAMPLES

74
x 2

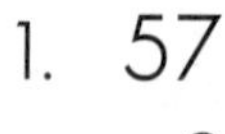

1 / 4	/ 8

148

23
x 7

1 / 4	2 / 1

161

46
x 9

3 / 6	5 / 4

414

1. 57 x 2
2. 74 x 8
3. 57 x 5
4. 79 x 3
5. 86 x 9
6. 53 x 7
7. 13 x 4
8. 74 x 6
9. 35 x 3
10. 52 x 8
11. 34 x 5
12. 95 x 9
13. 69 x 4

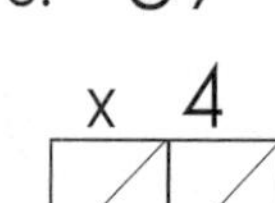

14. 27 x 6

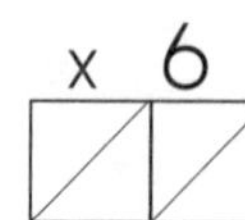

15. 73 x 2

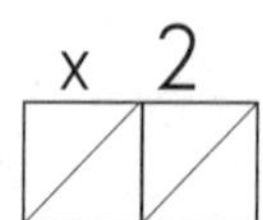

16. 62 x 7

MORE PRACTICE

Explain why you can find the correct product using this strategy.

Name ______________________ Date __________

More Place Value Boxes

Multiplying 2-Digit Numbers

Directions: Follow the directions in the example to use place value boxes to solve each problem.

1. 83 x 14 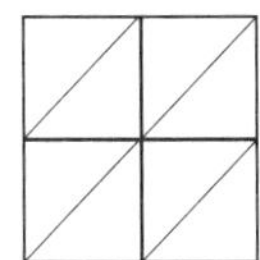

2. 98 x 26 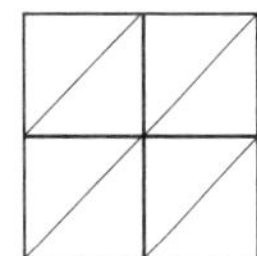

3. 34 x 32 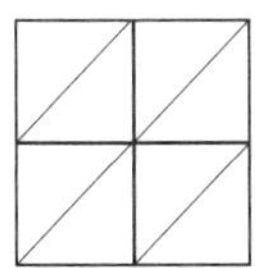

4. 57 x 48 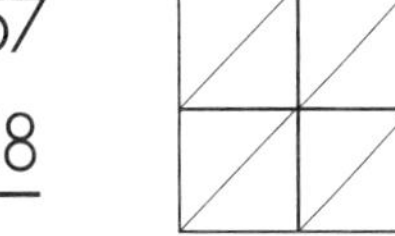

5. 87 x 44 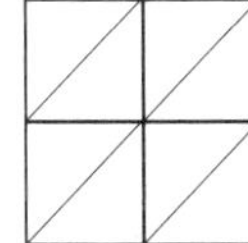

6. 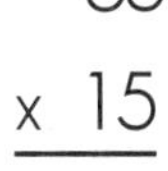 65 x 15 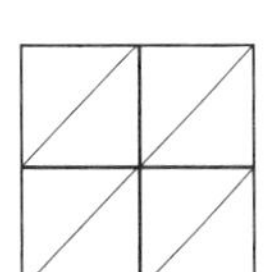

7. 79 x 63 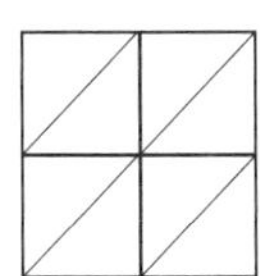

8. 43 x 22 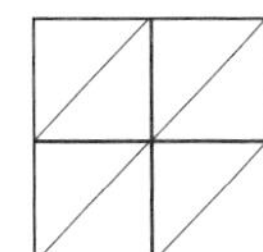

Example

Write the first factor across the top of the boxes and the second factor along the side.

59 x 48

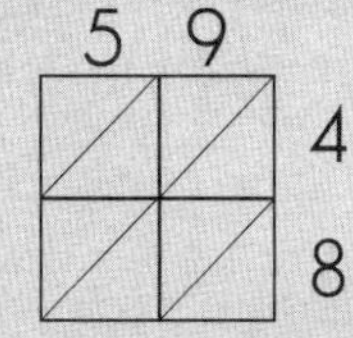

Multiply. Write the product of each pair of digits in the intersecting box.

5 9
2/0 3/6 4
4/0 7/2 8

Add along the diagonals. Regroup when necessary.

5 9
2/0 3/6 4
4/0 7/2 8

2,832

NAME ______________________ DATE __________

MULTIPLICATION

BIGGER BOXES

MULTIPLYING 3-DIGIT NUMBERS

Directions: Use place value boxes to solve each problem.

EXAMPLE

798
x 234

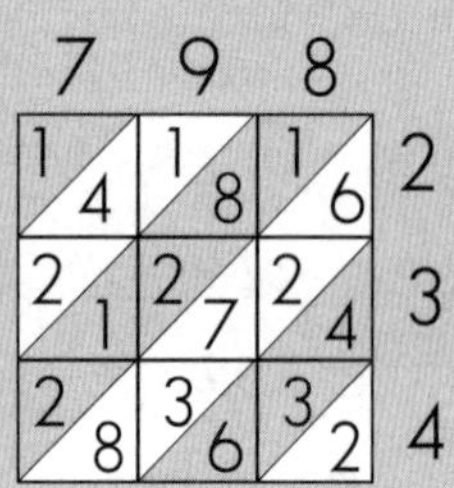

186,732

1. 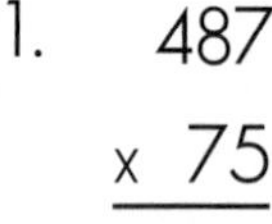
487
x 75

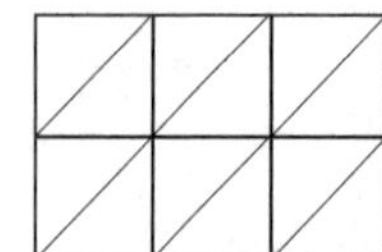

2. 519
x 91

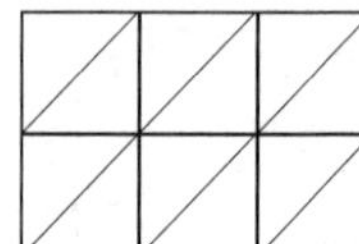

3. 718
x 601

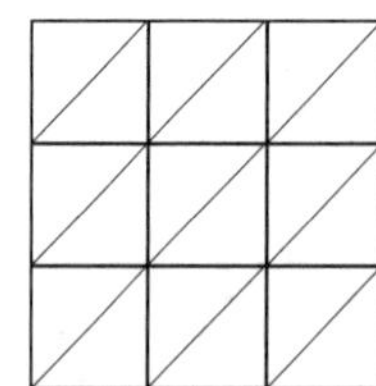

4. 924
x 627

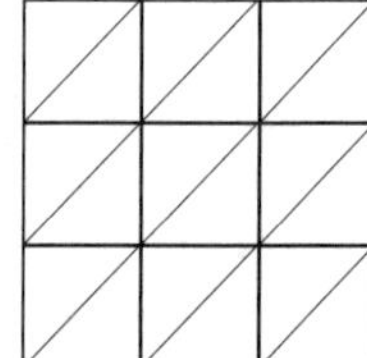

5. 812
x 354

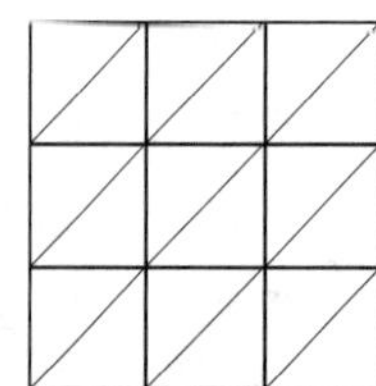

6. 643
x 352

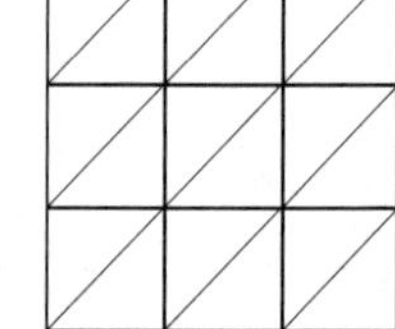

7. 276
x 198

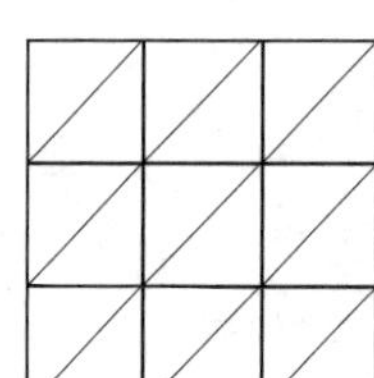

8. 
654
x 485

NAME ______________________ DATE __________

PLACE VALUE MATCH-UP

MULTIPLICATION

MULTIPLYING BY 1-DIGIT NUMBERS

Directions: Match each problem with its place value picture. Some values may need to be regrouped. Write the product under each problem.

32	28	214	130	2,436	3,015
x 5	x 6	x 3	x 7	x 2	x 4

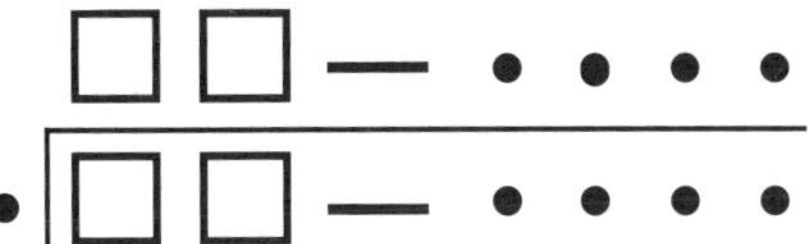

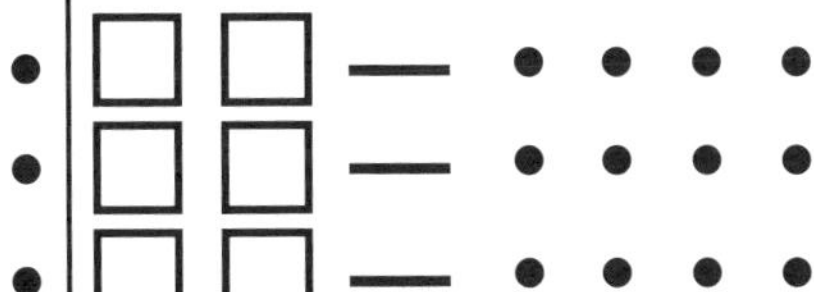

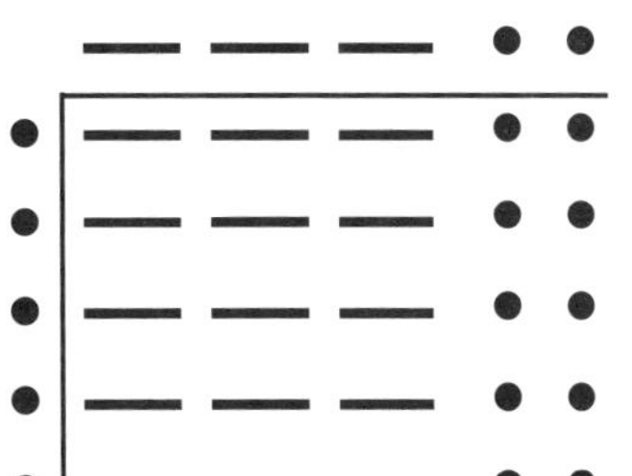

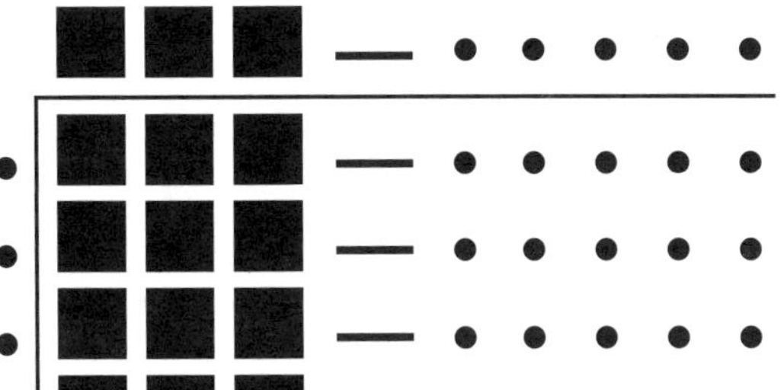

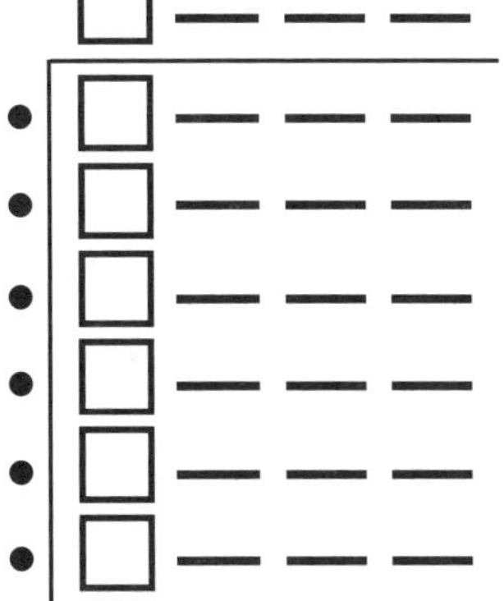

EXAMPLE

■ = 1,000 □ = 100

— = 10 • = 1

$$\begin{array}{r} 42 \\ \times\ 5 \\ \hline 210 \end{array}$$

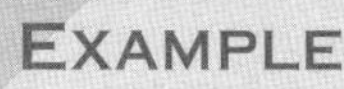

(20 tens and 10 ones)

MORE PRACTICE

Draw place value pictures for the following problems: 57 x 9, 41 x 7, 458 x 2, 187 x 5, and 576 x 9. Show your work on another sheet of paper.

Name ______________________ Date __________

Place Value Multiplication

Multiplying 2-Digit Numbers

Directions: Match each problem with its place value picture. Some values may need to be regrouped. Write the product under each problem.

53	32	215	51	22	352
x 20	x 40	x 30	x 34	x 16	x 12

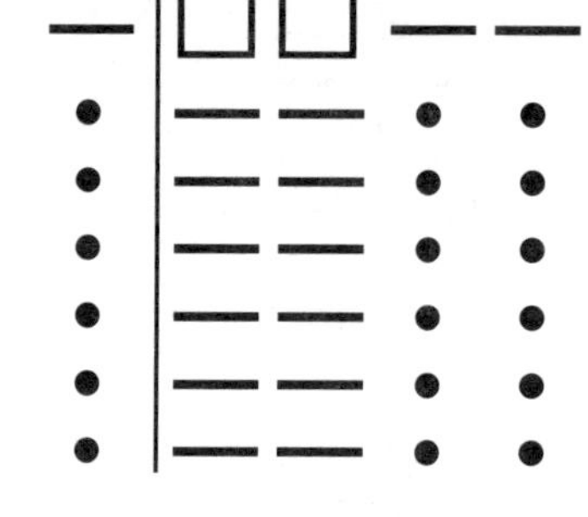

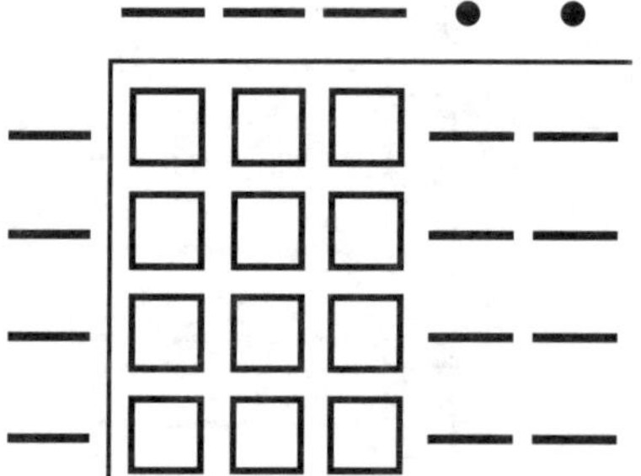

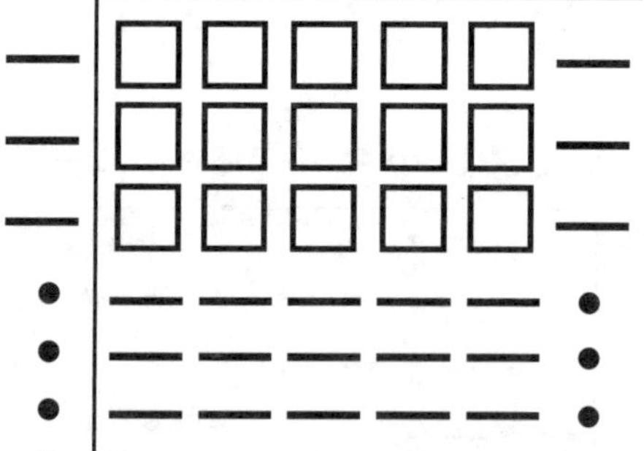

Example

■ = 1,000 □ = 100

— = 10 • = 1

$$\begin{array}{r} 221 \\ \times\ 20 \\ \hline 4{,}420 \end{array}$$

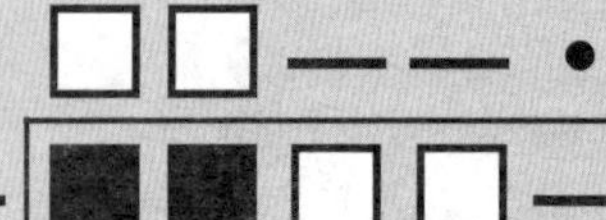

Intersecting symbols are multiplied. Therefore, a rod intersecting an open square is a filled square (10 x 100 = 1,000), a rod intersecting a rod is an open square, and so on.

More Practice

Draw place value pictures for the following problems: 47 x 30, 163 x 40, 54 x 32, and 682 x 13. Show your work on another sheet of paper.

NAME ______________________ DATE __________

REFLECTIONS ON MATH

MULTIPLICATION

COMMUTATIVE PROPERTY

Directions: Find each product. Then, switch the order of the factors, rewrite the problem, and solve. Answer the questions below.

1. 26 x 5 ____ x ____

2. 39 x 3 ____ x ____

3. 62 x 8 ____ x ____

4. 28 x 6 ____ x ____

5. 72 x 9 ____ x ____

6. 83 x 8 ____ x ____

7. 57 x 4 ____ x ____

8. 39 x 7 ____ x ____

9. 65 x 5 ____ x ____

10. 32 x 9 ____ x ____

11. 78 x 2 ____ x ____

12. 64 x 3 ____ x ____

13. 116 x 6 ____ x ____

14. 236 x 4 ____ x ____

15. 153 x 5 ____ x ____

16. 106 x 7 ____ x ____

How does the order of the factors affect the product? ______________________

____

Why might you choose to reorder the factors? ______________________

____

NAME ______________________ DATE __________

MULTIPLICATION

ROMAN NUMERALS

MULTIPLYING 1-DIGIT BY 3-DIGIT NUMBERS

Directions: Change the Roman numerals to standard numerals. Solve. Then, rewrite the product using Roman numerals.

EXAMPLE

I = 1

V = 5

X = 10

L = 50

C = 100

D = 500

M = 1,000

* On this page, • will be used for the multiplication symbol.

1. IV • CCXXXVIII =

2. III • CXXXV =

3. II • CCCXXIV =

4. IX • CV =

5. V • CXLVI =

6. VI • CCLI =

7. IV • DLXVIII =

8. IX • CCLXXIII =

9. VII • CLXIX =

10. VI • CDXIV =

11. V • DCXLV =

12. VIII • CDXLIV =

Name ______________________ Date __________

In the Box

MULTIPLICATION

Multiplying 2-Digit Numbers

Directions: Solve. Write the products in the puzzle. Show your work on another sheet of paper.

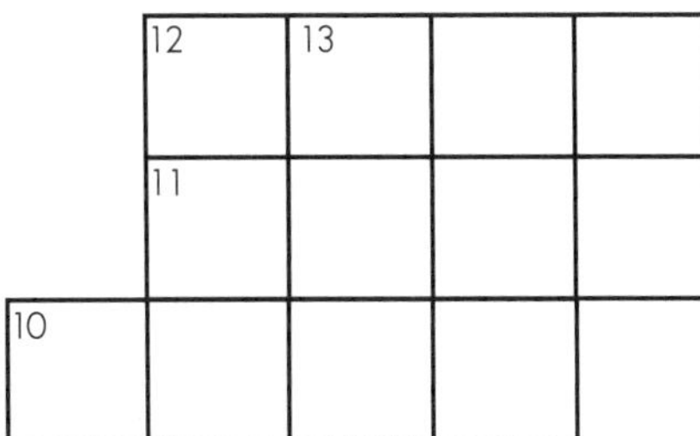

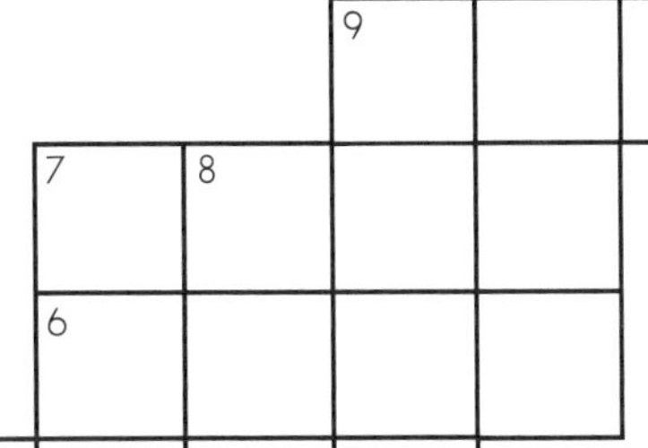

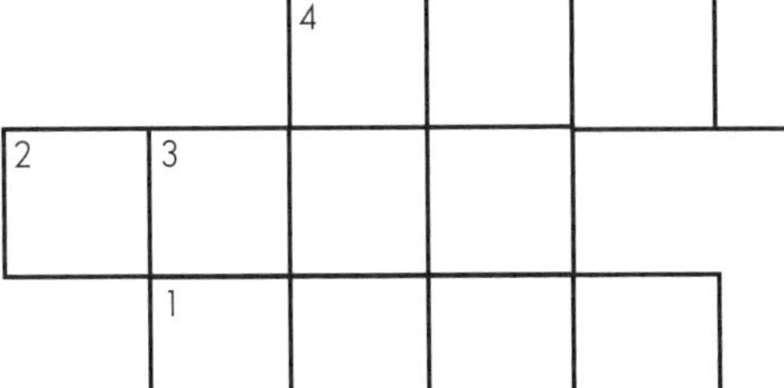

Across

1. 73 x 54
2. 92 x 62
4. 24 x 47
5. 95 x 16
6. 73 x 98
7. 99 x 22
9. 41 x 92
10. 95 x 33
11. 92 x 48
12. 78 x 42

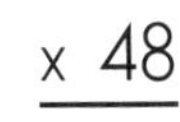

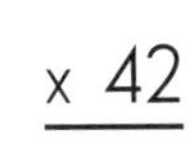

Down

3. 75 x 98
4. 52 x 21
5. 22 x 52
7. 86 x 22
8. 47 x 24
9. 75 x 50
10. 88 x 43
12. 51 x 67
13. 64 x 38

Name ______________________ Date __________

Finding the Right Tarp

MULTIPLICATION

Multiplying 2-Digit Numbers

Directions: Find the area of each tarp by multiplying its length and width. Show your work. Label your answers in square units. Then, follow the directions below.

28 units × 16 units

53 units × 37 units

41 units × 24 units

40 units × 40 units

59 units × 75 units

37 units × 17 units

84 units × 57 units

52 units × 18 units

Ty needs a tarp between 4,500 square units and 5,000 square units. Draw a triangle inside it.

Cara needs a tarp greater than 400 square units and less than 450 square units. Circle it.

Jack needs the smallest tarp greater than 1,000 square units. Draw a star inside it.

Kiki needs the smallest tarp with no side smaller than 50 units. Draw a heart inside it.

Name ______________________ Date __________

Multiplication

Gone Fishing

Multiplying 2-Digit Numbers

Directions: Solve each problem. Round the product to the nearest hundred. Shade the fish with the rounded answers to "catch" them.

67 x 53	46 x 31	23 x 95	43 x 93	63 x 12	80 x 26
53 x 18	34 x 13	50 x 17	78 x 14	99 x 57	19 x 12
64 x 58	62 x 61			95 x 66	71 x 69

400 4,900 3,800 3,600 200 2,200 300 3,700 2,100 8,700 1,000 1,100 2,000 800 900 4,000 6,300 1,400 1,500 7,000 5,600 600

NAME ______________________ DATE __________

MULTIPLICATION

STEPPING UP

PRACTICE

Directions: Start at the bottom. Multiply adjacent numbers. Write the product in the space above the factors. Continue until you reach the top.

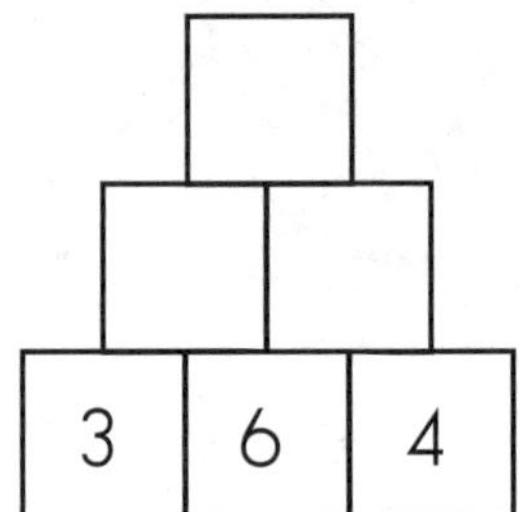

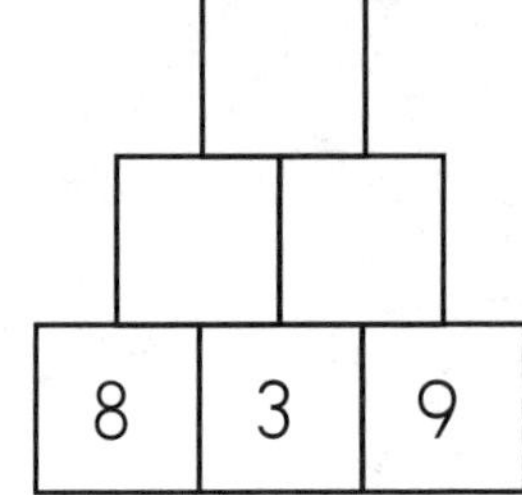

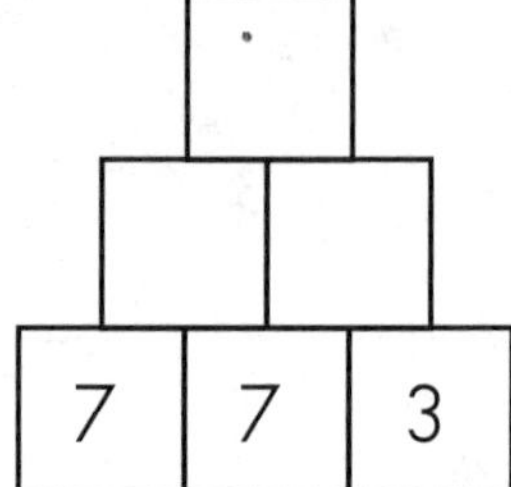

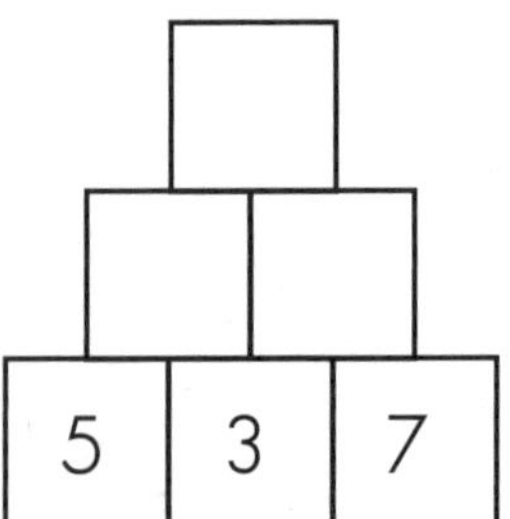

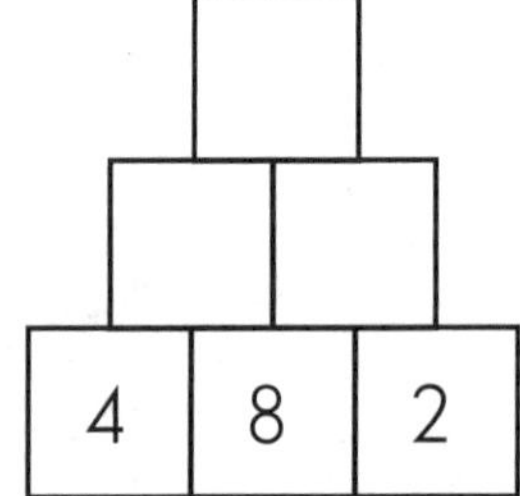

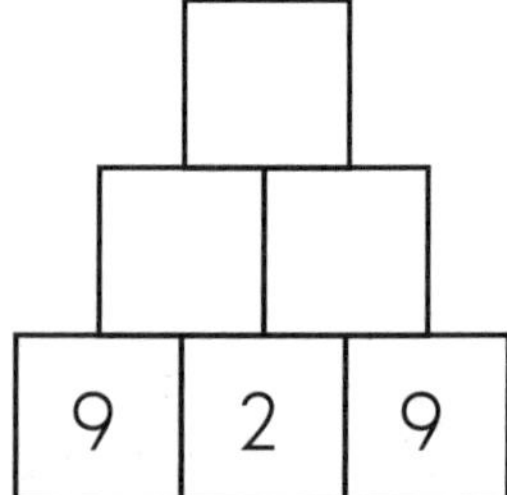

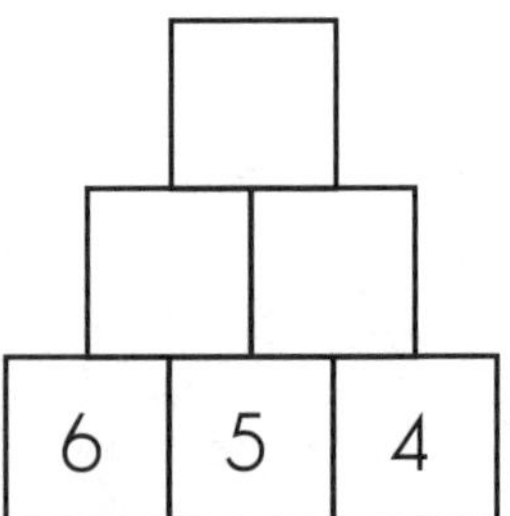

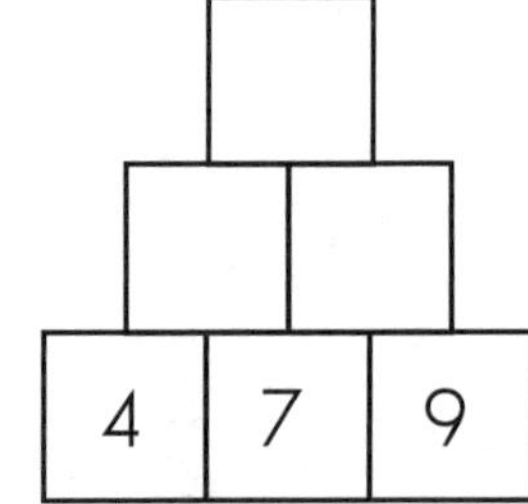

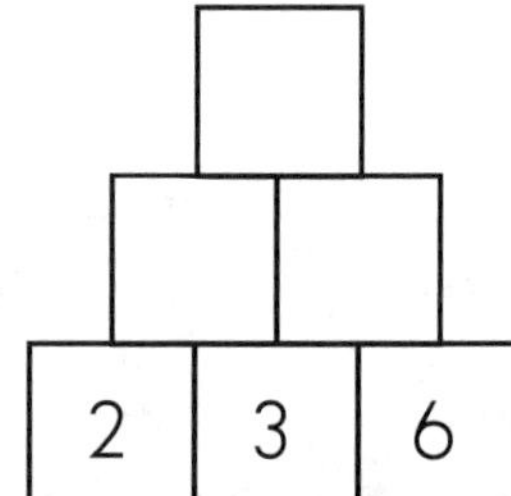

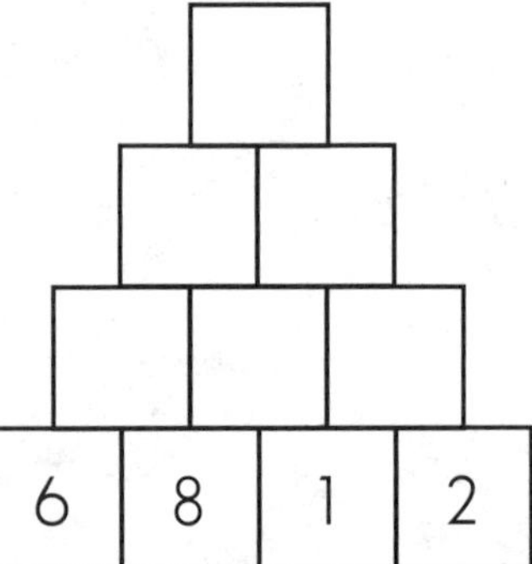

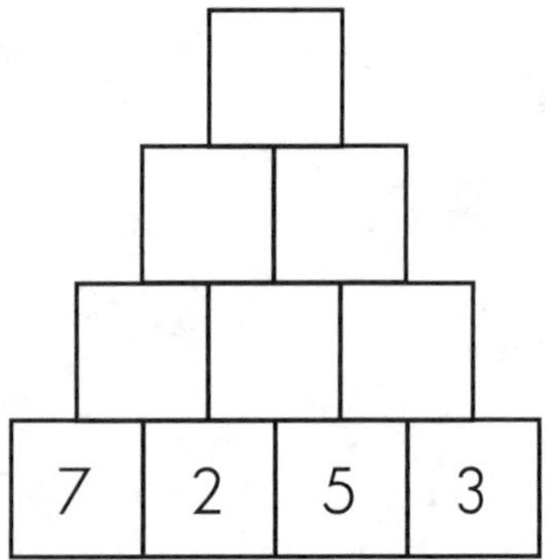

4 9 2 5

Name ____________________ Date __________

Careful Placement

MULTIPLICATION

Multiplying 3-Digit Numbers

Directions: Solve. One answer has been placed in the puzzle. Each of the other products has a place in the puzzle. Find each spot and fit each in.

312 × 311	542 × 494	745 × 588
686 × 139	598 × 234	610 × 349
544 × 427	842 × 719	515 × 366

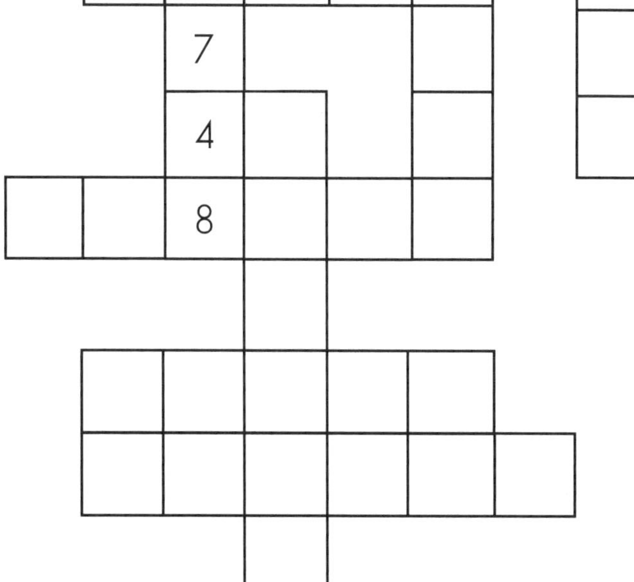

Name ______________________ Date __________

Place Value Strategy

1-Digit Divisors

Directions: Match the division problem with its place value picture. Write the quotient above each problem.

$2\overline{)112}$ $4\overline{)168}$ $5\overline{)235}$ $3\overline{)1{,}023}$ $4\overline{)616}$

Example

■ = 1,000 □ = 100

— = 10 • = 1

$3\overline{)102}$

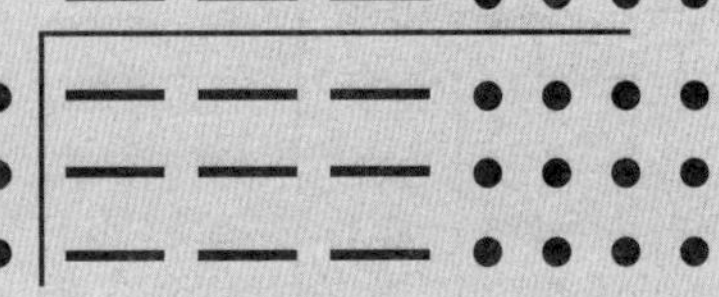

The divisor is shown along the left side. The dividend is broken apart in equal parts beside the divisor. You may have to regroup to make it work. For example, above a ten was regrouped into ten ones.

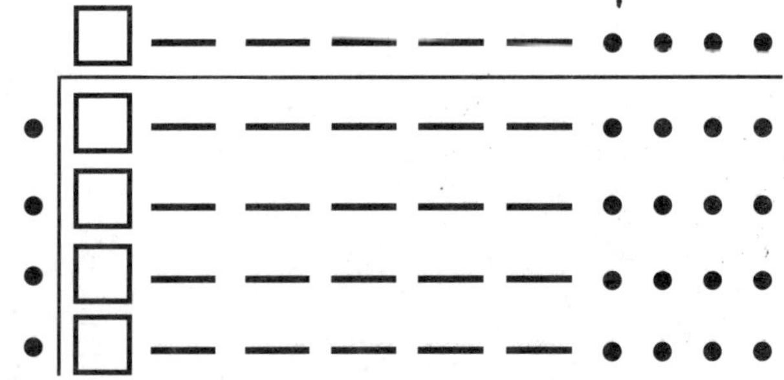

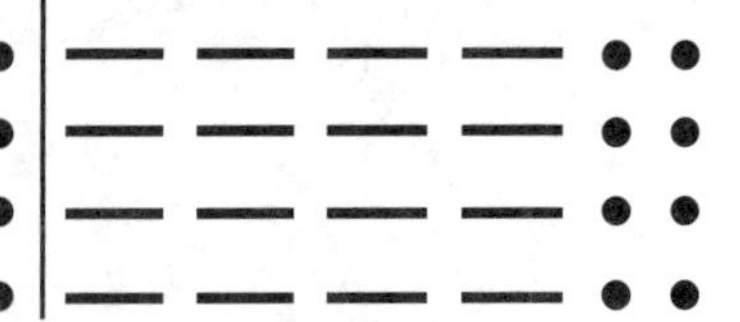

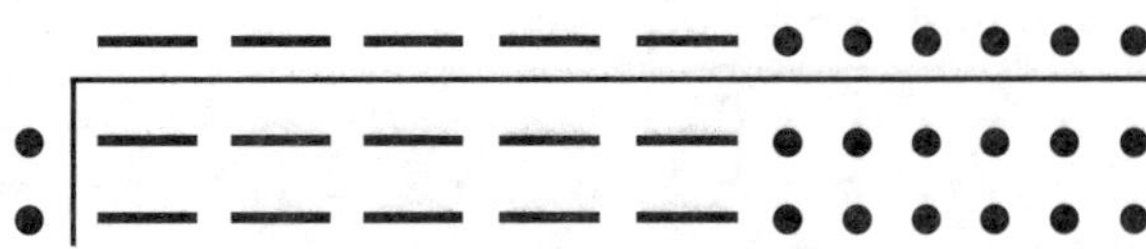

More Practice

Draw place value pictures for the following problems: 164 ÷ 4, 120 ÷ 5, 166 ÷ 2, 1,012 ÷ 4, and 486 ÷ 3. Show your work on another sheet of paper.

NAME ______________________________ DATE __________

DIVISION MATCH-UP

2-DIGIT DIVISORS

Directions: Match the division problem with its place value picture. Write the quotient above each problem.

$30\overline{)630}$ $40\overline{)6,200}$ $41\overline{)287}$ $24\overline{)528}$ $32\overline{)9,984}$

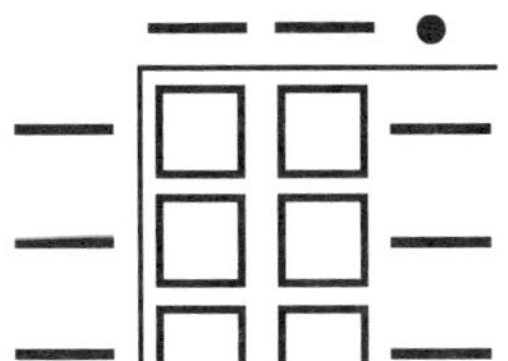

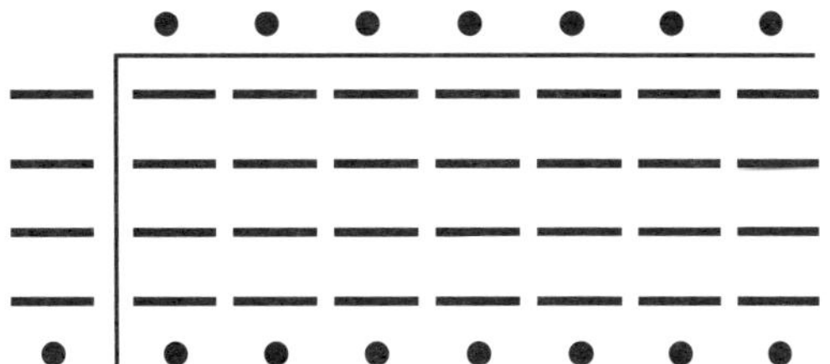

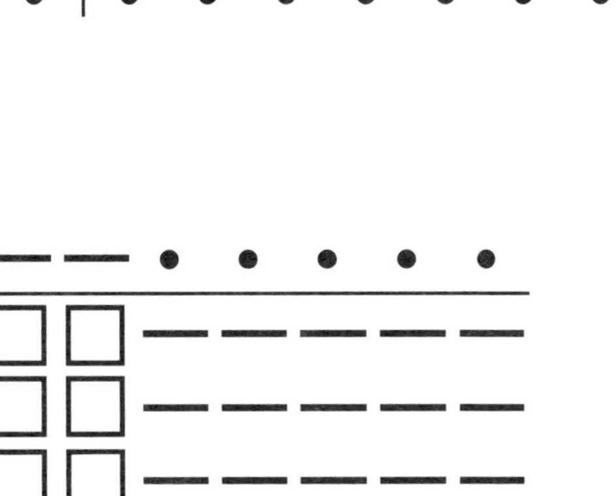

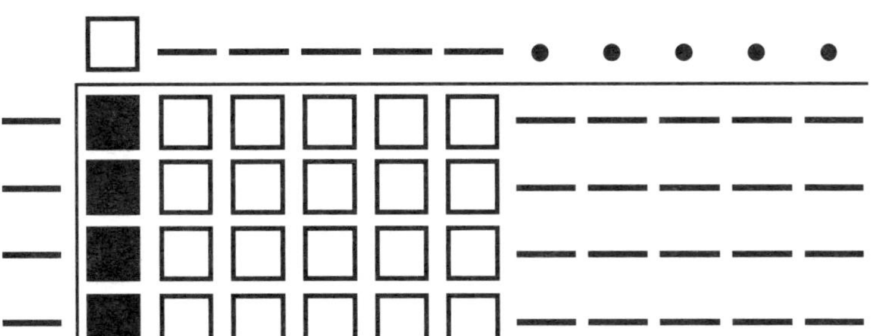

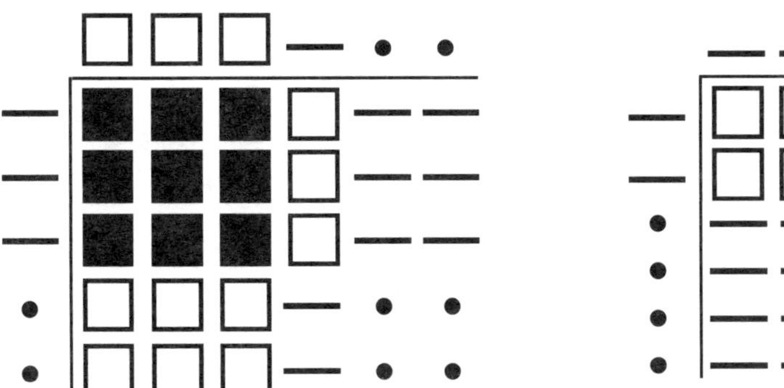

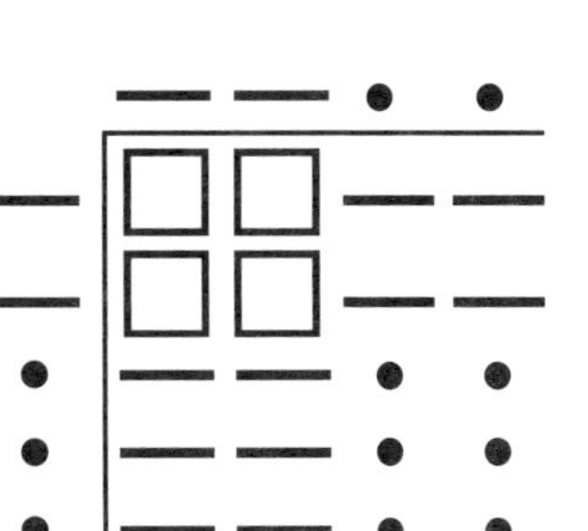

EXAMPLE

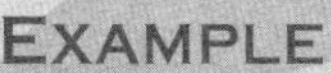

$21\overline{)693}$

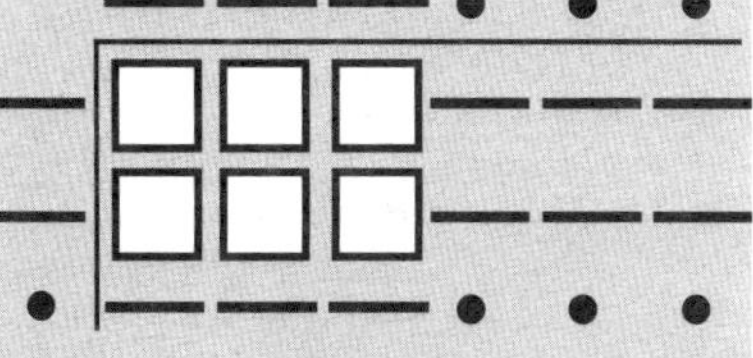

The divisor is shown along the left side. The dividend is broken apart in equal parts beside the divisor. You may need to regroup to make it work out evenly.

MORE PRACTICE

Draw place value pictures for the following problems: 150 ÷ 5, 315 ÷ 5, 290 ÷ 2, 1,220 ÷ 4, and 267 ÷ 3. Show your work on another sheet of paper.

Name ______________________ Date __________

Subtraction Strategy

DIVISION

1-Digit Divisors

Directions: Solve each problem using the subtraction strategy.

1. $2\overline{)52}$
2. $6\overline{)72}$
3. $3\overline{)114}$
4. $8\overline{)296}$
5. $6\overline{)576}$
6. $7\overline{)665}$
7. $7\overline{)728}$
8. $3\overline{)807}$
9. $9\overline{)4,617}$

Example

Division is like repeated subtraction. Looking for subtractable pieces is a great division strategy. When you put the pieces together, you find the quotient.

$$
\begin{array}{r|r}
285 & \\
2\overline{)570} & \\
-\ 400 & 200 \\
\hline
170 & \\
-\ 160 & 80 \\
\hline
10 & \\
-\ 10 & 5 \\
\hline
0 &
\end{array}
$$

(200 + 80 + 5 = 285)

More Practice

Circle all of the even quotients. Add them. Subtract 100 from the sum. This is the number of Earth days equivalent to one solar day on Mercury.

NAME ____________________ DATE __________

Subtract It Again

2-Digit Divisors

Directions: Solve each problem using the subtraction strategy.

1. $73\overline{)438}$

2. $18\overline{)828}$

3. $22\overline{)946}$

4. $51\overline{)969}$

5. $39\overline{)2,145}$

6. $63\overline{)756}$

7. $23\overline{)3,703}$

8. $16\overline{)5,232}$

9. $49\overline{)833}$

Example

Division is like repeated subtraction. Looking for subtractable pieces is a great division strategy. When you put the pieces together, you find the quotient.

$$\begin{array}{r|r} 32 & \\ 21\overline{)672} & \\ -630 & 30 \\ \hline 42 & \\ -42 & 2 \\ \hline 0 & \end{array}$$

(30 + 2 = 32)

NAME ______________________ DATE __________

BIGGER NUMBERS

3-DIGIT DIVISORS

Directions: Solve each problem using the subtraction strategy.

EXAMPLE

Division is like repeated subtraction. Looking for subtractable pieces is a great division strategy. When you put the pieces together, you find the quotient.

```
      672
132)88,704 |
   -66,000 | 500
    22,704 |
   -13,200 | 100
     9,500 |
    -6,600 |  50
     2,904 |
    -2,640 |  20
       264 |
      -264 |   2
         0 |
```

(500 + 100 + 50 + 20 + 2 = 672)

1. 315)3,780
2. 148)4,884
3. 258)11,610
4. 525)6,825
5. 148)5,328
6. 732)19,764
7. 215)66,865
8. 456)165,072
9. 279)41,013

NAME ______________________ DATE __________

SHORT DIVISION

1-DIGIT DIVISORS

Directions: Solve each problem using the strategy shown in the example.

1. $7\overline{)2{,}548}$

2. $4\overline{)2{,}916}$

3. $3\overline{)10{,}716}$

4. $9\overline{)5{,}643}$

5. $8\overline{)13{,}072}$

6. $6\overline{)165{,}816}$

7. $2\overline{)547{,}838}$

8. $9\overline{)759{,}078}$

EXAMPLE

"Long division" can be shortened by multiplying and subtracting in your head. Subtract, write the remainder beside the next digit, and continue.

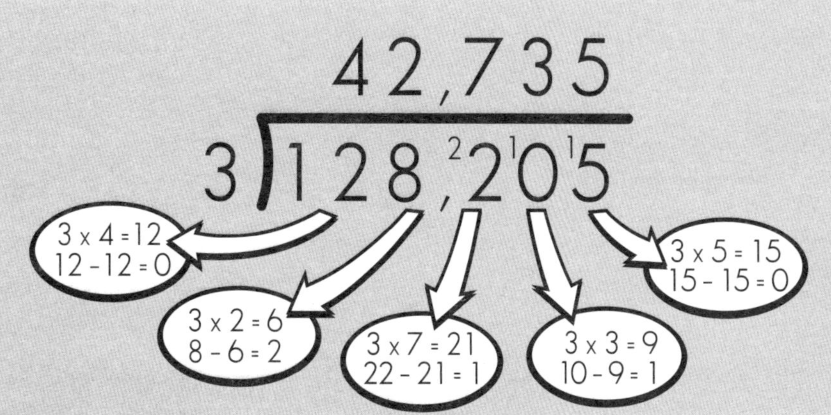

NAME ______________________ DATE __________

DIVISION

REMEMBERING REMAINDERS

1-DIGIT DIVISORS (WITH REMAINDERS)

Directions: Solve each problem using the short division strategy from page 33. Remember to include any remainder in your answer.

1. $2\overline{)757}$

2. $3\overline{)2,193}$

3. $8\overline{)5,235}$

4. $5\overline{)8,969}$

5. $4\overline{)20,074}$

6. $9\overline{)7,583}$

7. $7\overline{)22,856}$

8. $5\overline{)1,922}$

9. $2\overline{)5,834}$

10. $6\overline{)15,790}$

11. $8\overline{)10,581}$

12. $9\overline{)4,575}$

Name ______________________ Date __________

Play MATHO!

Division

Practice

Directions: Solve each problem. Cross out the quotients on the MATHO cards. The winning card will have five in a row.

$6\overline{)108}$ $9\overline{)441}$ $2\overline{)170}$ $5\overline{)125}$ $6\overline{)402}$

$9\overline{)486}$ $3\overline{)114}$ $5\overline{)355}$ $4\overline{)384}$ $8\overline{)216}$

$7\overline{)581}$ $8\overline{)456}$ $5\overline{)210}$ $3\overline{)237}$ $2\overline{)130}$

M	A	T	H	O
94	43	27	65	34
42	18	49	57	24
68	83	85	16	54
79	36	55	71	74
98	67	96	38	25

M	A	T	H	O
43	67	94	83	18
57	98	34	38	68
42	49	54	71	55
16	74	79	24	36
96	25	65	27	85

M	A	T	H	O
83	24	25	79	85
34	57	16	64	65
18	94	67	68	54
98	38	49	42	43
96	55	27	36	71

NAME ____________________ DATE __________

ROMAN NUMERALS

1-DIGIT DIVISORS

Directions: Change the Roman numerals to standard numerals. Solve. Then, rewrite the quotient using Roman numerals.

EXAMPLE

I = 1

V = 5

X = 10

L = 50

C = 100

D = 500

M = 1,000

1. DCCLXXV ÷ V =

2. CCLXXIII ÷ III =

3. DCLXXXII ÷ II =

4. DCLXXVI ÷ IV =

5. CMXX ÷ VIII =

6. MMCDXXXVI ÷ VI =

7. MMMCCXLIX ÷ IX =

8. MCCCLXXXVI ÷ VII =

9. MMMCDLVI ÷ IV =

10. MMMDCCXLV ÷ V =

11. MMCIV ÷ VIII =

12. MMCDLXVI ÷ IX =

Name ____________________ Date __________

Tic-Tac-Toe

DIVISION

Practice

Directions: Solve each problem. Use another sheet of paper to show your work. Play by drawing an O on each odd answer and an X on each even answer.

$4\overline{)552}$	$8\overline{)632}$	$9\overline{)783}$
$2\overline{)632}$	$2\overline{)804}$	$3\overline{)963}$
$5\overline{)670}$	$4\overline{)584}$	$8\overline{)392}$

$35\overline{)385}$	$19\overline{)722}$	$16\overline{)928}$
$15\overline{)960}$	$21\overline{)819}$	$43\overline{)473}$
$22\overline{)308}$	$44\overline{)572}$	$18\overline{)342}$

$5\overline{)4,615}$	$4\overline{)2,512}$	$19\overline{)8,322}$
$28\overline{)2,072}$	$9\overline{)2,277}$	$33\overline{)3,828}$
$7\overline{)1,183}$	$6\overline{)1,242}$	$84\overline{)7,980}$

$53\overline{)4,823}$	$31\overline{)682}$	$4\overline{)2,332}$
$29\overline{)957}$	$7\overline{)392}$	$81\overline{)1,134}$
$2\overline{)148}$	$9\overline{)3,582}$	$6\overline{)222}$

Name ______________________ Date __________

Start with the Remainder

Division

Practice

Directions: Solve and use the remainder of the previous problem as the divisor for the next problem. The last remainder times 21 should match the first divisor.

1. 84)5,873
2.)3,001
3.)3,143
4.)1,830
5.)4,583
6.)1,134
7.)2,797
8.)3,823
9.)971
10.)3,357
11.)1,565
12.)2,434
13.)1,457
14.)414
15.)1,557
16.)815
17.)1,527
18.)1,101
19.)312
20.)346

NAME ______________________ DATE __________

MIXED PRACTICE

AREA PROBLEMS

APPLICATION

Directions: Solve each problem. Show your work.

1. The lunch room is 50 feet by 35 feet. How many square feet is the lunchroom?

2. Jacquelyn wants to plant flowers. She can choose between a spot that is 24 inches by 78 inches or one that is 32 inches by 65 inches. She wants to use the location with the largest area. Which should she choose?

3. Each package of dough mix makes 400 square inches of pastry. Evan is making 3 inch by 6 inch rectangles of dough for a special recipe. He wants to make 24 rectangles. Is one package of dough enough? Explain.

4. Elieas has two sheets of construction paper. One sheet is 7 inches by 14 inches. The second is 8 inches by 13 inches. He wants to use the sheet with the largest area. Which one should he use?

5. Karen has a piece of fabric that is 16 inches by 42 inches. She wants to cut it into four pieces equal in area. How many square inches will each piece be?

6. Ms. Clay, the art teacher, made a mural from square tiles. There are 27 tiles in the top row and 39 tiles in the first column. How many tiles are in the mural? Tiles come in packages of 25. How many packages were purchased for the mural?

NAME ______________________ DATE __________

MIXED PRACTICE

FIND THE VOLUME

APPLICATION

Directions: Find the volume of each container. Show your work and label your answers with cubic units. Remember: volume = length x width x height.

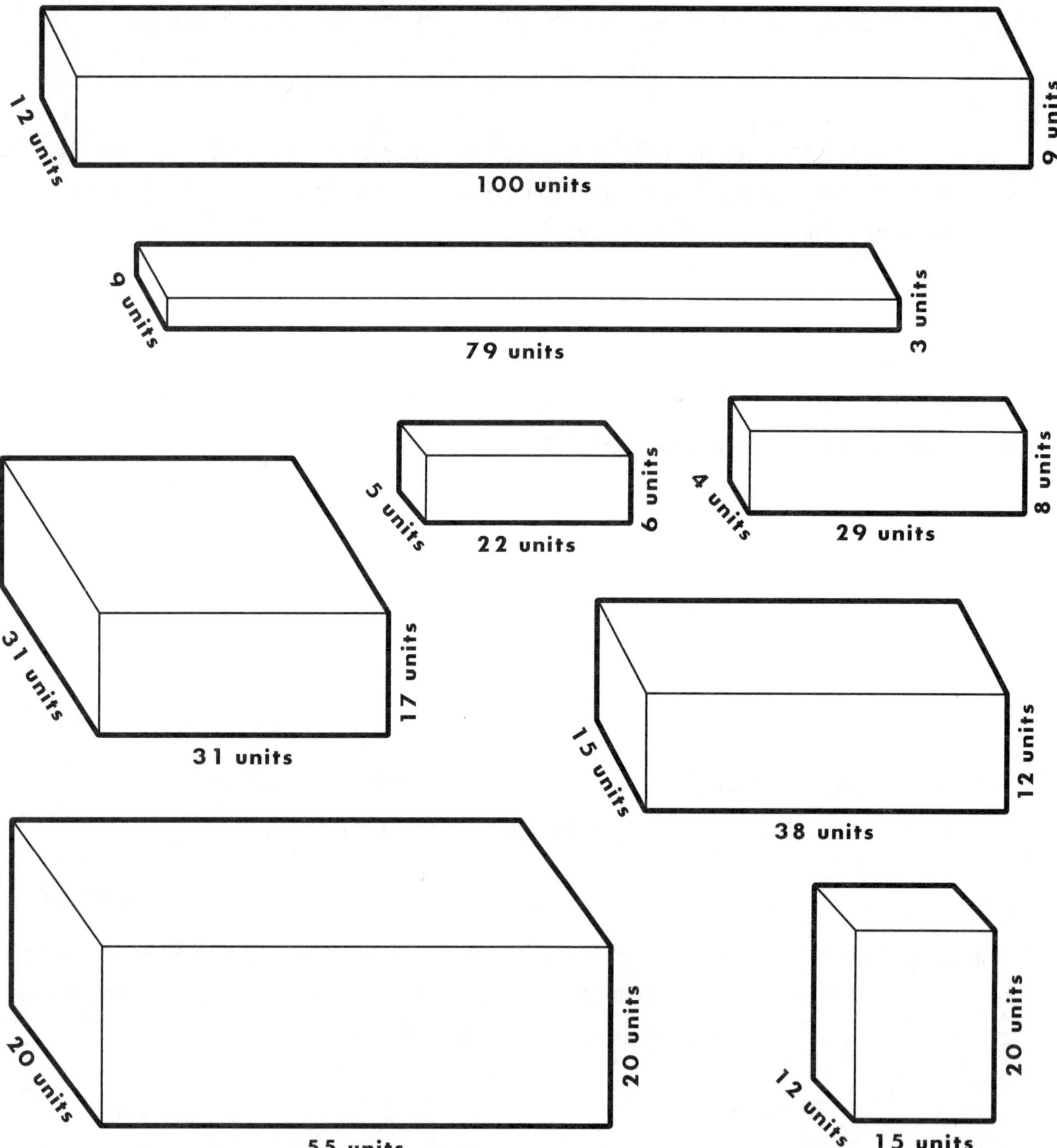

NAME ______________________________ DATE __________

MULTISTEP STORY PROBLEMS

MIXED PRACTICE

APPLICATION

Directions: Read carefully to solve each problem. Draw pictures, tables, or diagrams to help find the answers. Show your work and label your answers.

1. Zoe was allowed to bring two bags with five toys in each to the beach. She packed four bags with four toys in each. How many toys does she need to leave at home?

2. Graham has 25 nickels, 17 dimes, and 12 quarters. He plans to put an equal number of coins in each of 7 boxes. How many coins will he put in each box?

3. Georgia's popcorn and cookie order costs 4 quarters. She has 9 nickels and 5 dimes. Does she have enough money to pay for her order? By how much is she over or under?

4. Ian has 40 trading cards. He wants to put them into 5 equal piles. How many cards can he put in each pile? He bought the cards in packages of 20. Each pack cost $1.76. How many packs did he buy? How much did they cost altogether?

5. Shelica is selling three different kinds of cookies. If she sells them all, she will earn $5.07. She priced 25 at 5¢ each, 41 at 8¢ each, and the rest at 6¢ each. How many is she selling for 6¢?

6. Going Nutty, a store that sells nuts in bulk, sells almonds for $3.05 a pound. If they sold 60 five-pound bags of almonds, how much money did they make?

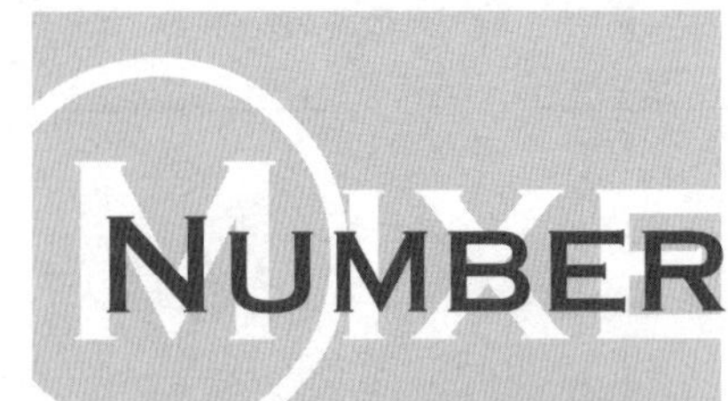

NAME ____________________ DATE __________

NUMBER RIDDLES

PRACTICE

Directions: Read carefully to solve each number riddle.

1. If you divide me into 36 equal parts, you get 52. What number am I?
2. If you multiply me by 19, you get 228. What number am I?
3. If you multiply me by 23, then add 44, you get 1,217. What number am I?
4. If you divide 646 by me, you get 17. What number am I?
5. If you add 11 to me, then divide by 13, you get 7. What number am I?
6. If you multiply me by 20, subtract 18, and divide by 63, you get 14. What number am I?
7. If you multiply me by 29, subtract 15, then divide by 18, you get 33. What number am I?
8. If you add 5 times 58 to me and divide by 29, you get 40. What number am I?
9. If you divide me by 47, add 2, and multiply by 11, you get 517. What number am I?
10. If you add 9 to me, then multiply by 16, you get 288. What number am I?
11. If you divide me by 39, subtract 6, then divide by 7, you get 8. What number am I?
12. If you multiply me by 73, add 64, multiply by 19, then divide by 76, you get 16. What number am I?
13. If you subtract 67 from me, divide by 15, then divide by 21, you get 3. What number am I?

NAME ______________________ DATE __________

END-OF-BOOK TEST

REVIEW

Directions: Answer each question.

1. Which of the following is not a multiple of 8?

   a. 24 b. 48 c. 72 d. 54

2. Which of the following is a multiple of 7?

   a. 24 b. 49 c. 37 d. 62

3. If 54 bracelets each have 38 beads. How many beads are there in all?

4. If 5,356 gum balls are put into 13 packages, how many gum balls are in each package?

5. Which multiplication problem is shown by this picture?

   a. 113 x 21 = 2,263 c. 21 x 113 = 2,373

   b. 21 x 103 = 2,163 d. 123 x 13 = 1,599

6. What division problem is shown by the picture?

   a. 2,373 ÷ 21 = 113 c. 1,599 ÷ 13 = 123

   b. 2,263 ÷ 113 = 21 d. 2,377 ÷ 113 = 21

7. Which of the following describe this array?

   a. 6 + 6 + 6 + 6 = 24 c. 4 groups of 6 equal 24

   b. 4 x 6 = 24 d. all of the above

8. Which of the following do not describe this array?

   a. 9 ÷ 3 = 3 c. 27 ÷ 3 = 9

   b. 9 x 3 = 27 d. all of the above

9. 8 x 40 = 10. 5 x 300 = 11. 7 x 900 =

12. 2700 ÷ 90 = 13. 560 ÷ 8 = 14. 16,000 ÷ 400 =

NAME ______________________ DATE __________

END-OF-BOOK TEST

15. $9 \times 56 =$

16. $47 \times 625 =$

17. $72 \times 38 =$

18. $284 \times 169 =$

19. $10{,}875 \div 29 =$

20. $648 \div 18 =$

21. $47{,}244 \div 254 =$

22. $1{,}116 \div 4 =$

23. What numbers belong in the following boxes?

a. b. c. d.

24. What is the product of 486 and 394?

4	8	6	
1 / 2	2 / a.	1 / 8	3
3 / b.	7 / 2	c. / 4	9
1 / 6	d. / 2	2 / 4	4

25. The area of a rectangle is 864 square units. How long could the sides be?
   a. 8 units by 108 units
   b. 24 units by 36 units
   c. 9 units by 96 units
   d. all of the above

26. The following problems are a fact family: $41 \times 20 = 820$, $20 \times 41 = 820$, $41 \div 20 = 820$, $820 \div 41 = 20$. True or false?

27. In the problem $392 \div 14 = 28$, 28 is the dividend. True or False?

28. In the problem $62 \times 34 = 2{,}108$, 62 is a factor. True or false?

Answer Key

Page 5

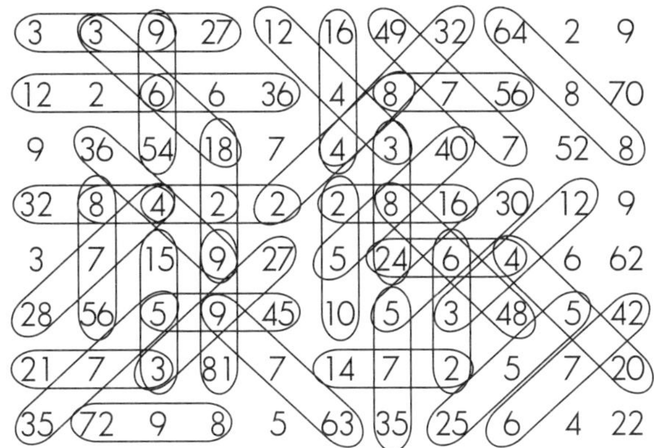

All options shown above: equations will vary.

Page 6

1. 3 x 9 = 27, 9 x 3 = 27, 27 ÷ 3 = 9, 27 ÷ 9 = 3;
2. 5 x 6 = 30, 6 x 5 = 30, 30 ÷ 5 = 6, 30 ÷ 6 = 5;
3. 4 x 7 = 28, 7 x 4 = 28, 28 ÷ 4 = 7, 28 ÷ 7 = 4;
4. 7 x 2 = 14, 2 x 7 = 14, 14 ÷ 7 = 2, 14 ÷ 2 = 7;
5. 9 x 4 = 36, 4 x 9 = 36, 36 ÷ 9 = 4, 36 ÷ 4 = 9;
6. 5 x 3 = 15, 3 x 5 = 15, 15 ÷ 5 = 3, 15 ÷ 3 = 5;
7. 8 x 9 = 72, 9 x 8 = 72, 72 ÷ 8 = 9, 72 ÷ 9 = 8;
8. 7 x 6 = 42, 6 x 7 = 42, 42 ÷ 7 = 6, 42 ÷ 6 = 7

Page 7

1. 8; 2. 5; 3. 18; 4. 7; 5. 8; 6. 3; 7. 7; 8. 24; 9. 32; 10. 9; 11. 1; 12. 4; 13. 14; 14. 7; 15. 4; 16. 6; 17. 3; 18. 5; 19. 42; 20. 8

Page 8

1. multiply each amount by 2; 2. 6 x 7 = 42 raisins; 3. 7 x 4 = 28 pieces of vanilla cookie; 4. 2 x 2 = 4, 4 x 9 = 36 nuts; 5. multiply each amount by 8: 1 x 8 = 8 candy-coated chocolate pieces, 2 x 8 = 16 handfuls of nuts, 3 x 8 = 24 tablespoons of oat cereal, 4 x 8 = 32 teaspoons of candy corn, 5 x 8 = 40 tablespoons of other cereal, 6 x 8 = 48 tablespoons of raisins, 7 x 8 = 56 vanilla cookies, 8 x 8 = 64 pretzels, 9 x 8 = 72 dried apricots

Page 9

Game 1: Mikaela: 3 x 4 = 12, 3 x 2 = 6, 3 x 6 = 18, 3 x 4 = 12, 3 x 5 = 15; 12 + 6 + 18 + 12 + 15 = 63 (final score); Jeremy: 3 x 3 = 9, 3 x 1 = 3, 3 x 6 = 18, 3 x 4 = 12, 3 x 2 = 6; 9 + 3 + 18 + 12 + 6 = 48 (final score)

Page 9 (continued)

Game 2: Mikaela: 5 x 3 = 15, 5 x 1 = 5, 5 x 5 = 25, 5 x 2 = 10, 5 x 5 = 25; 15 + 5 + 25 + 10 + 25 = 80 (final score); Jeremy: 5 x 5 = 25, 5 x 2 = 10, 5 x 6 = 30, 5 x 1 = 5, 5 x 4 = 20; 25 + 10 + 30 + 5 + 20 = 90 (final score)

Game 3: Mikaela: 4 x 6 = 24, 4 x 1 = 4, 4 x 4 = 16, 4 x 3 = 12, 4 x 3 = 12; 24 + 4 + 16 + 12 + 12 = 68 (final score); Jeremy: 4 x 2 = 8, 4 x 5 = 20, 4 x 4 = 16, 4 x 2 = 8, 4 x 1 = 4; 8 + 20 + 16 + 8 + 4 = 56 (final score)

Game 4 : Mikaela: 2 x 5 = 10, 2 x 2 = 4, 2 x 4 = 8, 2 x 2 = 4, 2 x 3 = 6; 10 + 4 + 8 + 4 + 6 = 32 (final score); Jeremy: 2 x 6 = 12, 2 x 1 = 2, 2 x 4 = 8, 2 x 3 = 6, 2 x 2 = 4; 12 + 2+ 8 + 6 + 4 = 32 (final score)

Game 5: Mikaela: 6 x 5 = 30, 6 x 2 = 12, 6 x 4 = 24, 6 x 1 = 6, 6 x 6 = 36; 30 + 12 + 24 + 6 + 36 = 108 (final score); Jeremy: 6 x 3 = 18, 6 x 2 = 12, 6 x 6 = 36, 6 x 2 = 12, 6 x 5 = 30; 18 + 12 + 36 + 12 + 30 = 108 (final score)

Game 6: Mikaela: 3 x 3 = 9, 3 x 2 = 6, 3 x 1 = 3, 3 x 6 = 18, 3 x 6 = 18; 9 + 6 + 3 + 18 + 18 = 54 (final score); Jeremy: 3 x 4 = 12, 3 x 4 = 12, 3 x 2 = 6, 3 x 5 = 15, 3 x 1 = 3; 12 + 12 + 6 + 15 + 3 = 48 (final score)

Page 10

1. 4 groups of 8 tens and 6 ones, 86 + 86 + 86 + 86 = 344;
2. 3 groups of 7 tens and 4 ones, 74 + 74 + 74 = 222;
3. 2 groups of 9 tens and 3 ones, 93 + 93 = 186;
4. 4 groups of 5 tens and 1 one, 51 + 51 + 51 + 51 = 204;
5. 6 groups of 3 tens and 5 ones, 35 + 35 +35 +35 + 35 +35 = 210
6. 4 groups of 2 tens and 2 ones, 22 + 22 + 22 + 22 = 88;
7. 5 groups of 4 tens and 7 ones, 47 + 47 + 47 +47 + 47 = 235;
8. 3 groups of 3 hundreds, 8 tens and 2 ones, 382 + 382 + 382 = 1,146;
9. 2 groups of 2 hundreds, 6 tens, and 9 ones, 269 + 269 = 538;
10. 6 groups of 1 hundred, 4 tens, and 4 ones, 144 + 144 + 144 + 144 + 144 + 144 = 864;
11. 5 groups of 4 hundreds, 2 tens, and 8 ones, 428 + 428 + 428 + 428 + 428 = 2,140;
12. 4 groups of 5 hundreds, 4 tens, and 7 ones, 547 + 547 + 547 + 547 = 2,188

ANSWER KEY

Page 11
1. 45; 450; 4,500; 2. 21; 210; 2,100; 3. 48; 480; 4,800; 4. 36; 360; 3,600; 5. 49; 490; 4,900; 6. 24; 240; 2,400; 7. 32; 320; 3,200; 8. 6; 60; 600; 9. 720; 10. 1,000; 11. 160; 12. 450; 13. 5,600; 14. 180; 15. 1,800; 16. 630

Page 12
1. 9 x 1 = 9, 9 x 80 = 720; 720 + 9 = 729; 2. 3 x 7 = 21, 3 x 50 = 150; 150 + 21 = 171; 3. 6 x 8 = 48, 6 x 70 = 420; 420 + 48 = 468; 4. 2 x 5 = 10, 2 x 60 = 120; 120 + 10 = 130; 5. 4 x 2 = 8, 4 x 30 = 120; 120 + 8 = 128; 6. 7 x 6 = 42, 7 x 50 = 350, 350 + 42 = 392; 7. 5 x 1 = 5, 5 x 80 = 400; 400 + 5 = 405; 8. 6 x 7 = 42, 6 x 60 = 360; 360 + 42 = 402; 9. 7 x 9 = 63; 7 x 30 = 210; 210 + 63 = 273; 10. 8 x 0 = 0, 8 x 30 = 240, 240 + 0 = 240; 11. 5 x 1 = 5, 5 x 20 = 100; 100 + 5 = 105; 12. 3 x 8 = 24, 3 x 80 = 240; 240 + 24 = 264; 13. 9 x 9 = 81, 9 x 70 = 630; 630 + 81 = 711, 14. 4 x 5 = 20, 4 x 60 = 240; 240 + 20 = 260; 15. 7 x 9 = 63, 7 x 80 = 560; 560 + 63 = 623

Page 13
2 x 4 = 8; 2 x 20 = 40; 80 x 4 = 320; 80 x 20 = 1,600; 8 + 20 + 320 + 1,600 = 1,968;
6 x 1 = 6; 6 x 50 = 300; 40 x 1 = 40; 40 x 50 = 2,000; 6 + 300 + 40 + 2,000 = 2,346;
7 x 3 = 21; 7 x 40 = 280; 40 x 3 = 120; 40 x 40 = 1,600; 21 + 280 + 120 + 1,600 = 2,021;
3 x 2 = 6; 3 x 80 = 240; 20 x 2 = 40, 20 x 80 = 1,600; 6 + 240 + 40 + 1,600 = 1,886
2 x 5 = 10; 2 x 60 = 120; 90 x 5 = 450; 90 x 60 = 5,400; 10 + 120 + 450 + 5,400 = 5,980;
6 x 7 = 42; 6 x 30 = 180; 50 x 7 = 350; 50 x 30 = 1,500; 42 + 180 + 350 + 1,500 = 2,072;
1 x 4 = 4; 1 x 90 = 90; 70 x 4 = 280; 70 x 90 = 6,300; 4 + 90 + 280 + 6,300 = 6,674;
3 x 8 = 24; 3 x 60 = 180; 10 x 8 = 80; 10 x 60 = 600; 24 + 180 + 80 + 600 = 884;
6 x 7 = 42; 6 x 70 = 420; 20 x 7 = 140; 20 x 70 = 1,400; 42 + 420 + 140 + 1,400 = 2,002;
4 x 4 = 16; 4 x 10 = 40; 50 x 4 = 200; 50 x 10 = 500; 16 + 40 + 200 + 500 = 756

Page 14
1. 6 x 71 = 426; 30 x 71 = 2,130; 426 + 2,130 = 2,556; 2. 6 x 58 = 348; 40 x 58 = 2,320; 348 + 2,320 = 2,668;

Page 14 (continued)
3. 5 x 42 = 210; 30 x 42 = 1,260; 210 + 1,260 = 1,470; 4. 6 x 19 = 114; 80 x 19 = 1,520; 114 + 1,520 = 1,634; 5. 9 x 93 = 837; 40 x 93 = 3,720; 837 + 3,720 = 4,557; 6. 7 x 38 = 266; 20 x 38 = 760; 266 + 760 = 1,026; 7. 3 x 24 = 72; 60 x 24 = 1,440; 72 + 1,440 = 1,512; 8. 4 x 99 = 396; 50 x 99 = 4,950; 396 + 4,950 = 5,396; 9. 2 x 65 = 130; 70 x 65 = 4,550; 130 + 4,550 = 4,680; 10. 4 x 37 = 148; 10 x 37 = 370; 148 + 370 = 518; 11. 6 x 43 = 258; 90 x 43 = 3,870; 258 + 3,870 = 4,128; 12. 3 x 72 = 216; 20 x 72 = 1,440; 216 + 1,440 = 1,656

Page 15
1. 5 x 606 = 3,030; 90 x 606 = 54,540; 3,030 + 54,540 = 57,570; 2. 2 x 350 = 700; 70 x 350 = 24,500; 700 + 24,500 = 25, 200; 3. 8 x 490 = 3,920; 10 x 490 = 4,900; 3,920 + 4,900 = 8,820; 4. 3 x 861 = 2,583; 40 x 861 = 34,440; 2,583 + 34,440 = 37,023; 5. 1 x 907 = 907; 50 x 907 = 45,350; 907 + 45,350 = 46,257; 6. 6 x 831 = 4,986; 80 x 831 = 66,480; 100 x 831 = 83,100; 4,986 + 66,480 + 83,100 = 154,566; 7. 6 x 347 = 2,082; 10 x 347 = 3,470; 200 x 347 = 69,400; 2,082 + 3,470 + 69,400 = 74,952; 8. 1 x 257 = 257; 50 x 257 = 12,850; 700 x 257 = 179,900; 257 + 12,850 + 179,900 = 193,007; 9. 6 x 946 = 5,676; 10 x 946 = 9,460; 900 x 946 = 851,400; 5,676 + 9,460 + 851,400 = 866,536; 10. 6 x 895 = 5,370; 500 x 895 = 447,500; 5,370 + 447,500 = 452,870

Page 16
1. 10, 14, 114; 2. 56, 32, 592; 3. 25, 35, 285; 4. 21, 27, 237; 5. 72, 54, 774; 6. 35, 21, 371; 7. 4, 12, 52; 8. 42, 24, 444; 9. 9, 15, 105; 10. 40, 16, 416; 11. 15, 20, 170; 12. 81, 45, 855; 13. 24, 36, 276; 14. 12, 42, 162; 15. 14, 6, 141; 16. 42, 14, 434

Page 17
1. 8, 3, 32, 12; 1,162; 2. 18, 16, 54, 48; 2,558; 3. 9, 12, 6, 8; 1,088; 4. 20, 28, 40, 56; 2,736; 5. 32, 28, 32, 28; 3,828; 6. 6, 5, 30, 25; 975; 7. 42, 54, 21, 27; 4,977; 8. 8, 6, 8, 6; 946

Page 18
1. 28, 56, 49, 20, 40, 35; 36,525; 2. 45, 9, 81, 5, 1, 9; 47,229; 3. 42, 6, 48, 0, 0, 0, 7, 1, 8; 43,518; 4. 54, 12, 24, 18, 4, 8, 63, 14, 28; 579,348; 5. 24, 3, 6, 40, 5, 10, 32, 4, 8; 287, 448; 6. 18, 12, 9, 30, 20, 15, 12, 8, 6; 226,336; 7. 2, 7, 6, 18, 63, 54, 16, 56, 48; 54,648; 8. 24, 20, 16, 48, 40, 32, 30, 25, 20; 317,190

Answer Key

Page 19
32 x 5 = 160 (15 tens and 10 ones); 28 x 6 = 168 (12 tens and 48 ones); 214 x 3 = 642 (6 hundreds, 3 tens, and 12 ones); 130 x 7 = 910 (7 hundreds and 21 tens); 2,436 x 2 = 4,872 (2 thousands, 8 hundreds, 6 tens, and 12 ones); 3,015 x 4 = 12,060 (12 thousands, 4 tens, and 40 ones)

Page 20
53 x 20 = 1,060 (10 hundreds and 6 tens); 32 x 40 = 1,280 (12 hundreds and 8 tens); 215 x 30 = 6,450 (6 thousands, 3 hundreds, and 15 tens); 51 x 34 = 1,734 (15 hundreds, 23 tens, and 4 ones); 22 x 16 = 352 (2 hundreds, 14 tens, and 12 ones); 352 x 12 = 4,224 (3 thousands, 11 hundreds, 12 tens, and 4 ones)

Page 21
1. 130, 5 x 26 = 130; 2. 117, 3 x 39 = 117; 3. 496, 8 x 62 = 496; 4. 168, 6 x 28 = 168; 5. 648, 9 x 72 = 648; 6. 664, 8 x 83 = 664; 7. 228, 4 x 57 = 288; 8. 273, 7 x 39 = 273; 9. 325, 5 x 65 = 325; 10. 288, 9 x 32 = 288; 11. 156, 2 x 78 = 156; 12. 192, 3 x 64 = 192; 13. 696, 6 x 116 = 696; 14. 944, 4 x 236 = 944; 15. 765, 5 x 153 = 765; 16. 742, 7 x 106 = 742; Order of factors does not affect the product; Answers will vary

Page 22
1. 4 x 238 = 952: CMLII; 2. 3 x 135 = 405: CDV; 3. 2 x 324 = 648: DCXLVIII; 4. 9 x 105 = 945: CMXLV; 5. 5 x 146 = 730: DCCXXX; 6. 6 x 251 = 1,506: MDVI; 7. 4 x 568 = 2,272: MMCCLXXII; 8. 9 x 273 = 2,457: MMCDLVII; 9. 7 x 169 = 1,183: MCLXXXIII; 10. 6 x 414 =2,484: MMCDLXXXIV; 11. 5 x 645 = 3,225: MMMCCXXV; 12. 8 x 444 = 3,552: MMMDLII

Page 23
Across: 1. 3,942; 2. 5,704; 4. 1,128; 5. 1,520, 6. 7,154; 7. 2,178; 9. 3,772; 10. 3,135; 11. 4,416; 12. 3,276
Down: 3. 7,350; 4. 1,092; 5. 1,144; 7. 1,892; 8. 1,128; 9. 3,750; 10. 3,784; 12. 3,417; 13. 2,432

Page 24
28 x 16 = 448 square units; 53 x 37 = 1,961 square units; 41 x 24 = 984 square units; 40 x 40 = 1,600 square units; 37 x 17 = 629 square units; 59 x 75 = 4,425 square units; 84 x 57 = 4,788 square units; 52 x 18 = 936 square units; 28 x 16: circle; 40 x 40: star; 59 x 75: heart; 84 x 57: triangle

Page 25
row 1: 3,551; 1,426; 2,185; 3,999; 756; 2,080;
row 2: 954; 442; 850; 1,092; 5,643; 228;
row 3: 3,712; 3,782; 6,270; 4,899;
shade the following fish: 400; 4,900; 3,800; 3,600; 2,100; 200; 2,200; 3,700; 1,100; 800; 900; 4,000; 6,300; 1,400; 5,600

Page 26
from left to right and top to bottom: 3 x 6 = 18, 6 x 4 = 24, 18 x 24 = 432; 8 x 3 = 24, 3 x 9 = 27, 24 x 27 = 648; 7 x 7 = 49, 7 x 3 = 21, 49 x 21 = 1,029; 5 x 3 = 15, 3 x 7 = 21, 15 x 21 = 315; 4 x 8 = 32, 8 x 2 = 16, 32 x 16 = 512; 9 x 2 = 18, 2 x 9 = 18, 18 x 18 = 324; 6 x 5 = 30, 5 x 4 = 20, 30 x 20 = 600; 4 x 7 = 28, 7 x 9 = 63, 28 x 63 = 1,764; 2 x 3 = 6, 3 x 6 = 18, 6 x 18 = 108; 6 x 8 = 48, 8 x 1 = 8, 1 x 2 = 2, 48 x 8 = 384, 8 x 2 = 16, 384 x 16 = 6,144; 7 x 2 = 14, 2 x 5 = 10, 5 x 3 = 15, 14, x 10 = 140, 10 x 15 = 150, 140 x 150 = 21,000; 4 x 9 = 36, 9 x 2 = 18, 2 x 5 = 10, 36 x 18 = 648, 18 x 10 = 180, 648 x 180 = 116,640

Page 27
from left to right and top to bottom: 97,032; 267,748; 438,060; 95,354; 139,932; 212,890; 232,288; 605,398; 188,490; Across (top to bottom): 232,288; 97,032; 438,060; 95,354; 139,932; Down (left to right): 267,748; 605,398; 212,890; 188,490

Page 28
112 ÷ 2 = 56, two ones along left side/5 tens and six ones along top; 168 ÷ 4 = 42, 4 ones along left side/4 tens and 2 ones along top; 235 ÷ 5 = 47, 5 ones along left side/4 tens and 7 ones along top; 1,023 ÷ 3 = 341, 3 ones along left side/3 hundreds, 4 tens, and 1 one along top; 616 ÷ 4 = 154, 4 ones along left side/1 hundred, 5 tens, and 4 ones along top

Page 29
630 ÷ 30 = 21, 3 tens along the left side/ two tens and 1 one along top; 6,200 ÷ 40 = 155, 4 tens along left side/1 hundred, 5 tens, and 5 ones along top; 287 ÷ 41 = 7, 4 tens and 1 one along left side/7 ones along top; 528 ÷ 24 = 22, 2 tens and 4 ones along left side/2 tens and 2 ones along top; 9,984 ÷ 32 = 312, 3 tens and 2 ones along left side/3 hundreds, 1 ten, and 2 ones along top

Answer Key

Page 30
1. 26; 2. 12; 3. 38; 4. 37; 5. 96; 6. 95; 7. 104; 8. 269; 9. 513; Subtraction strategies will vary

Page 31
1. 6; 2. 46; 3. 43; 4. 19; 5. 55; 6. 12; 7. 161; 8. 327; 9. 17; Subtraction strategies will vary

Page 32
1.12; 2. 33; 3. 45; 4. 13; 5. 36; 6. 27; 7. 311; 8. 362; 9. 147; Subtraction strategies will vary

Page 33
1. 364; 2. 729; 3. 3,572; 4. 627; 5. 1,634; 6. 27,636; 7. 273,919; 8. 84,343

Page 34
1. 387 R1; 2. 731; 3. 654 R3; 4. 1,793 R4; 5. 5,018 R2; 6. 842 R5; 7. 3,265 R1; 8. 384 R2; 9. 2,917; 10. 2,631 R4; 11. 1,322 R5; 12. 508 R3

Page 35
from left to right and top to bottom: 18; 49; 85; 25; 67; 54; 38; 71; 96; 27; 83; 57; 42; 79; 65

Page 36
1. 775 ÷ 5 = 155: CLV; 2. 273 ÷ 3 = 91: XCI 3. 682 ÷ 2 = 341: CCCXLI; 4. 676 ÷ 4 = 169: CLXIX; 5. 920 ÷ 8 = 115: CXV; 6. 2,436 ÷ 6 = 406: CDVI; 7. 3,249 ÷ 9 = 361: CCCLXI; 8. 1,386 ÷ 7 = 198: CXCVIII; 9. 3,456 ÷ 4 = 864: DCCCLXIV; 10. 3,745 ÷ 5 = 749: DCCXLIX; 11. 2,104 ÷ 8 = 263: CCLXIII; 12. 2,466 ÷ 9 = 274: CCLXXIV

Page 37
from left to right and top to bottom in each game:
game 1: 138 (X), 79 (O), 87 (O), 316 (X), 402 (X), 321 (O), 134 (X), 146 (X), 49 (O);
game 2: 11 (O), 38 (X), 58 (X), 64 (X), 39 (O), 11 (O), 14 (X), 13 (O), 19 (O);
game 3: 923 (O), 628 (X), 438 (X), 74 (X), 253 (O), 116 (X), 169 (O), 207 (O), 95 (O);
game 4: 91 (O), 22 (X), 583 (O), 33 (O), 33 (O), 56 (X), 14 (X), 74 (X), 398 (X), 37 (O)

Page 38
1. 69 R77; 2. 38 R75; 3. 41 R68; 4. 26 R62; 5. 73 R57; 6. 19 R51; 7. 54 R43; 8. 88 R38; 9. 24 R35; 10. 95 R32; 11. 48 R29; 12. 83 R27; 13. 52 R26; 14. 15 R24; 15. 64 R21; 16. 38 R17; 17. 89 R14; 18. 78 R9; 19. 34 R6; 20. 57 R4

Page 39
1. 50 x 35 = 1,750 square feet; 2. 24 x 78 = 1,872, 32 x 65 = 2,080, the 32" x 65" spot; 3. 3 x 6 = 18 square inches, 18 x 24 = 432 square inches, 432 > 400: one package will not be enough; 4. 7 x 14 = 98, 8 x 13 = 104, the 13" x 8" sheet; 5. 16 x 42 = 672, 672 ÷ 4 = 168 square inches per piece; 6. 27 x 39 = 1,053 tiles are in the mural, 1,053 ÷ 25 = 42 R3: 43 packages were purchased for the mural

Page 40
12 x 100 x 9 = 10,800 cubic units; 9 x 79 x 3 = 2,133 cubic units; 31 x 31 x 17 = 16,337 cubic units; 5 x 22 x 6 = 660 cubic units; 4 x 29 x 8 = 928 cubic units; 15 x 38 x 12 = 6,840 cubic units; 20 x 55 x 20 = 22,000 cubic units; 12 x 15 x 20 = 3,600 cubic units

Page 41
1. 2 x 5 = 10, 4 x 4 = 16, 16 - 10 = 6 toys; 2. 25 + 17 + 12 = 54, 54 ÷ 7 = 7 R5, 7 coins in each box with 5 left over; 3. 4 x $0.25 = $1.00, 9 x $0.05 = $0.45, 5 x $0.10 = $0.50, $0.45 + $0.50 = $0.95, she does not have enough money, under by 5 cents; 4. 40 ÷ 5 = 8 cards, 40 ÷ 20 = 2 packs, $1.76 x 2 = $3.52; 5. $0.25 x 5 = $1.25, 41 x $0.08 = $3.28, $1.25 + $3.28 = $4.53, $5.07 - $4.53 = $0.54, 54 ÷ 6 = 9 cookies at 6 cents each; 6. 5 x $3.05 = $15.25, $15.25 x 60 = $915.00

Page 42
1. 1,872; 2. 12; 3. 51; 4. 10,982; 5. 80; 6. 45; 7. 21; 8. 870; 9. 2,115; 10. 9; 11. 2,418; 12. 0; 13. 1,012

Pages 43–44
1. d; 2. b.; 3. 2,052 beads.; 4. 412; 5. c.; 6. a.; 7. d.; 8. a.; 9. 320; 10. 1,500; 11. 63,00; 12. 3; 13. 70; 14. 40; 15. 504; 16. 29,375; 17. 2,736; 18. 47,996; 19. 375; 20. 36; 21. 186; 22. 279; 23. a. 4, b. 6, c. 5, d. 3; 24. 191,484; 25. d.; 26. false; 27. false; 28. true